INTIMATE
MOMENTS
WITH THE
SAVIOR

*Learning
to love*

KEN GIRE

Intimate Moments with the Savior
Copyright © 1989 by Ken Gire

Daybreak Books are published by
the Zondervan Publishing House
1415 Lake Drive, S.E.,
Grand Rapids, Michigan 49506

Library of Congress Cataloging-in-Publication Data
Gire, Ken.
    Intimate moments with the Savior / by Ken Gire.
      p. cm.
    ISBN 0-310-21770-9
    1. Bible. N.T. Gospels—Meditations. 2. Jesus Christ—
Biography—Meditations. I. Title.
BS2555.4.G57   1989
232.9–dc20   89–11641
                                      CIP

Printed in the United States of America

89 90 91 92 93 / DH / 10 9 8 7 6 5 4 3

edicated to
Judy

For loving me all the way
from Ft. Worth to Aledo to Nacogdoches
to Poolville to Fullerton—
and for the confidence that you will love me
even to the ends of the earth.

For loving me as a student,
a pastor, an oilfield equipment salesman,
an aspiring writer, a wallpaper hanger,
an unemployed writer,
and, finally, as a professional writer.

For believing in me
initially, when there was not much to believe in,
and years later, when I no longer believed in myself.

For sacrificing even the cupboards
when all the cupboards were bare.

You have worn the millstone
of being married to a writer
as gracefully as a princess
would wear a diamond pendant.

If the readers of this book look back on it
with any measure of warmth and affection,
may they offer up a prayer of thanks
for you.

For without you
there would not be a writer,
let alone this book.

"Martha, Martha," the Lord answered,
"You are worried and upset
about many things . . ."

Contents

FOREWORD

Just keeping up with the torrid pace of daily responsibilities yields a heart full of worries and only a handful of rewards. Yet, strangely, we stay at it.

Forcing ourselves to deny the exacting toll such a hurry-up lifestyle takes on us, we are reluctant to face the hard fact that being busy is not a satisfactory substitute for being holy. On the contrary, racing through one week after another at breakneck speed leads to tragic consequences—shallow roots and superficial fruit. Worst of all, God gets only the leftovers because we formed the bad habit of operating on spiritual "empty."

We need help. What we really need is periodic moments to refuel and reflect, to weigh essential priorities against screaming demands. If we plan to stay strong in the race, the pit stops become increasingly more important. But let's be real about this. Life is not suddenly going to slow down and grant us a chunk of free time to recover. As beautiful as a six-month sabbatical of calm silence may sound, it isn't going to happen. Meditation marathons are things monks in a monastery may be able to enjoy, but hectic mothers in the kitchen or pressurized people in the workplace? Get serious.

To be painfully realistic, the best most folks can hope for is a few moments a day from which fresh perspective can be gleaned. That won't come from entertaining moments at the movies or from quick moments in the newspaper or from boring moments staring at late-night talk shows. What we need first and foremost are intimate moments with the Savior . . . time spent all alone with Him, watching His model, listening to His counsel, feeling His touch. We need some way to connect our temporal world with His eternal perspective.

Thanks to my gifted friend, Ken Gire, that critical need is no longer a tantalizing wish; it is now a tangible reality. The book you hold in your hand is all you need to add breadth and depth to an existence that has been shallow long enough. I can't think of anyone better qualified to help us make the most of these essential moments.

For years Ken and I have coauthored numerous study guides connected with my "Insight for Living" radio broadcasts. This has given him an opportunity to cultivate his style and, at the same time, given me an opportunity to pull up close and observe his skills. If there is such a thing as the gift of writing, it is my opinion that Ken Gire has it. Creative, colorful, lucid, and easy to read, he has developed a firm grip on this elusive craft, much of which cannot be taught. In athletic terms, the man's a natural.

Having sifted through his manuscript for several days, I feel not only better acquainted with the characters who crossed Jesus' path, but, much more importantly, I feel closer to the Savior himself. Nothing is more satisfying to my soul.

I am confident that *Intimate Moments with the Savior* will have a similar effect on you as well. As you set aside only a few minutes each day for successive first-century visits, you will find yourself pleasantly surprised with the result. Nothing will happen suddenly, but over the long haul you will discover changes taking place.

I cannot promise that life's torrid pace will be reduced or that all those demands on your time will be decreased, but somehow *you* will begin to change. These intimate moments will ultimately yield a heart full of rewards, giving you sufficient strength to handle your handful of worries.

Chuck Swindoll
Senior Pastor, Radio Bible Teacher, Author

XII

INTRODUCTION

Life is a kitchenful of preparations that has a tendency to distract the Martha in all of us. It is the purpose of this book to help bring us out of the kitchen for a few minutes to sit, with Mary, at the Savior's feet.

For there the words of Jesus wait so patiently to enter our hearts. There, in his presence, we learn to listen. There we learn to look into his eyes. And there we learn to love him.

Learning to love Jesus. That's what this book is all about. The best way to do that, I felt, was simply to show him to you. I have attempted to take you back in time to the intimate moments Jesus spent with individuals—to see what they saw, to hear what they heard, to feel what they felt. In those moments Jesus saw something in them that filled him with compassion. And in those moments they saw something in him that brought them to their knees.

The book is not designed to be read at one sitting. It is meant to be savored over a period of time, a portion here, a portion there. After waking up in the morning. Before going to bed at night. During a break at work. Before a walk. Whenever you hunger for the Savior's presence.

Each of these little portions of fellowship begins with a Bible reading. Growing out of that reading is a meditation, which gives the reader pause to reflect on that intimate moment. Out of the meditation branches a prayer. But you'll notice that the prayer doesn't end with the traditional Amen. That is because it is unfinished. You are invited to complete the prayer, bringing your own thoughts, your own feelings, your own burdens, your own petitions, your own praise.

With each intimate moment you spend at the Savior's feet, may you see him a little more clearly and love him a little more deeply than you did before you sat down.

Ken Gire

An
INTIMATE MOMENT
WITH
MARY AND JOSEPH

SCRIPTURE

In those days Caesar Augustus issued a decree that a census should be taken of the entire Roman world. (This was the first census that took place while Quirinius was governor of Syria.) And everyone went to his own town to register.

So Joseph also went up from the town of Nazareth in Galilee to Judea, to Bethlehem the town of David, because he belonged to the house and line of David. He went there to register with Mary, who was pledged to be married to him and was expecting a child. While they were there, the time came for the baby to be born, and she gave birth to her firstborn, a son. She wrapped him in cloths and placed him in a manger, because there was no room for them in the inn.

Luke 2:1–7

MEDITATION

For the census, the royal family has to travel eighty-five miles. Joseph walks, while Mary, nine months pregnant, rides sidesaddle on a donkey, feeling every jolt, every rut, every rock in the road.

By the time they arrive, the small hamlet of Bethlehem is swollen from an influx of travelers. The inn is packed, people feeling lucky if they were able to negotiate even a small space on the floor. Now it is late, everyone is asleep, and there is no room.

But fortunately, the innkeeper is not all shekels and mites. True, his stable is crowded with his guests' animals, but if they could squeeze out a little privacy there, they were welcome to it.

Joseph looks over at Mary, whose attention is concentrated on fighting a contraction. "We'll take it," he tells the innkeeper without hesitation.

The night is still when Joseph creaks open the stable door. As he does, a chorus of barn animals makes discordant note of the intrusion. The stench is pungent and humid, as there have not been enough hours in the day to tend the guests, let alone the livestock. A small oil lamp, lent them by the innkeeper, flickers to dance shadows on the walls. A disquieting place for a woman in the throes of childbirth. Far from home. Far from family. Far from what she had expected for her firstborn.

But Mary makes no complaint. It is a relief just to finally get off the donkey. She leans back against the wall, her feet swollen, back aching, contractions growing stronger and closer together.

Joseph's eyes dart around the stable. Not a minute to lose. Quickly. A feeding trough would have to make do for a crib. Hay would serve as a mattress. Blankets? Blankets? Ah, his robe. That would do. And those rags hung out to dry would help. A gripping contraction doubles Mary over and sends him racing for a bucket of water.

The birth would not be easy, either for the mother or the child. For every royal privilege for this son ended at conception.

A scream from Mary knifes through the calm of that silent night. Joseph returns, breathless, water sloshing from the wooden bucket. The top of the baby's head has already pushed its way into the world. Sweat pours from Mary's contorted face as Joseph, the most unlikely midwife in all Judea, rushes to her side.

The involuntary contractions are not enough, and Mary has to push with all her strength, almost as if God were refusing to come into the world without her help.

Joseph places a garment beneath her, and with a final push and a long sigh her labor is over.

The Messiah has arrived.

Elongated head from the constricting journey through the birth canal. Light skin, as the pigment would take days or even weeks to surface. Mucus in his ears and nostrils. Wet and slippery from the amniotic fluid. The Son of the Most High God umbilically tied to a lowly Jewish girl.

The baby chokes and coughs. Joseph instinctively turns him over and clears his throat.

Then he cries. Mary bares her breast and reaches for the shivering baby. She lays him on her chest, and his helpless cries subside. His tiny head bobs around on the unfamiliar terrain. This will be the first thing the infant-king learns. Mary can feel his racing heartbeat as he gropes to nurse.

Deity nursing from a young maiden's breast. Could anything be more puzzling—or more profound?

Joseph sits exhausted, silent, full of wonder.

The baby finishes and sighs, the divine Word reduced to a few unintelligible sounds. Then, for the first time, his eyes fix on his mother's. Deity straining to focus. The Light of the World, squinting.

Tears pool in her eyes. She touches his tiny hand. And hands that once sculpted mountain ranges cling to her finger.

She looks up at Joseph, and through a watery veil, their souls touch. He crowds closer, cheek to cheek with his betrothed. Together they stare in awe at the baby Jesus, whose heavy eyelids begin to close. It has been a long journey. The King is tired.

And so, with barely a ripple of notice, God stepped into the warm lake of humanity. Without protocol and without pretention.

Where you would have expected angels, there were only flies. Where you would have expected heads of state, there were only donkeys, a few haltered cows, a nervous ball of sheep, a tethered camel, and a furtive scurry of curious barn mice.

Except for Joseph, there was no one to share Mary's pain. Or her joy. Yes, there were angels announcing the Savior's arrival—but only to a band of blue-collar shepherds. And yes, a magnificent star shone in the sky to mark his birthplace—but only three foreigners bothered to look up and follow it.

Thus, in the little town of Bethlehem . . . that one silent night . . . the royal birth of God's Son tiptoed quietly by . . . as the world slept.

PRAYER

ear Jesus,

Though there was no room for you in the inn, grant this day that I might make abundant room for you in my heart. Though your own did not receive you, grant this hour that I may embrace you with open arms. Though Bethlehem overlooked you in the shuffle of the census, grant me the grace, this quiet moment, to be still and know that you are God. You, whose only palace was a stable, whose only throne was a feeding trough, whose only robes were swaddling clothes.

On my knees I confess that I am too conditioned to this world's pomp and pageantry to recognize God cooing in a manger.

Forgive me. Please. And help me understand at least some of what your birth has to teach—that divine power is not mediated through strength, but through weakness; that true greatness is not achieved through the assertion of rights, but through their release; and that even the most secular of things can be sacred when you are in their midst.

And for those times when you yearn for my fellowship and stand at the door and knock, grant me a special sensitivity to the sound of that knock so I may be quick to my feet. Keep me from letting you stand out in the cold or from ever sending you away to some stable. May my heart be warm and inviting, so that when you do knock, a worthy place will always be waiting. . . .

AN
INTIMATE MOMENT
WITH
NICODEMUS

SCRIPTURE

ow there was a man of the Pharisees named Nicodemus, a member of the Jewish ruling council. He came to Jesus at night and said, "Rabbi, we know you are a teacher who has come from God. For no one could perform the miraculous signs you are doing if God were not with him."

In reply Jesus declared, "I tell you the truth, no one can see the kingdom of God unless he is born again."

"How can a man be born when he is old?" Nicodemus asked. "Surely he cannot enter a second time into his mother's womb to be born!"

Jesus answered, "I tell you the truth, no one can enter the kingdom of God unless he is born of water and the Spirit. Flesh gives birth to flesh, but the Spirit gives birth to spirit. You should not be surprised at my saying, 'You must be born again.' The wind blows wherever it pleases. You hear its sound, but you cannot tell where it comes from or where it is going. So it is with everyone born of the Spirit."

"How can this be?" Nicodemus asked.

"You are Israel's teacher," said Jesus, "and do you not understand these things? I tell you the truth, we speak of what we know, and we testify to what we have seen, but still you people do not accept our testimony. I have spoken to you of earthly things and you do not believe; how then will you believe if I speak of heavenly things? No one has ever gone into heaven except the one who came from heaven—the Son of Man. Just as Moses lifted up the snake in the desert, so the Son of Man must be lifted up, that everyone who believes in him may have eternal life.

"For God so loved the world that he gave his one and only Son, that whoever believes in him shall not perish but have eternal life. For God did not send his Son into the world to condemn the world, but to save the world through him. Whoever believes in him is not condemned, but whoever does not believe stands condemned already because he has not believed in the name of God's one and only Son. This is the verdict: Light has come into the world, but men loved darkness instead of light because their deeds were evil. Everyone who does evil hates the light and will not come into the light for fear that his deeds will be exposed. But whoever lives by the truth comes into the light, so that it may be seen plainly that what he has done has been done through God."

John 3:1–21

MEDITATION

The resumé is impressive:

A Pharisee—one of the intellectual guardians of the Law.

Member of the Sanhedrin—the esteemed ruling council.

Israel's teacher—*the* authority, the one whose opinion could sway the vote, the one whose words were most quoted.

Most impressive. Nicodemus is at the top of the religious ladder, looking down.

But the view from the top is, at best, disappointing. And now, he steps down from that ladder to walk the streets. Searching.

He comes *at night.*

Two words between the lines in his resume that follow him through the Gospel like a stray. When John later describes him, he doesn't mention the credentials but rather this telling clue to his character: "Nicodemus, the man who earlier had visited Jesus *at night.*"

Thus, cloaked in darkness, Nicodemus wends his way through the side streets of Jerusalem . . . slowly . . . cautiously . . . every so often stepping into the shadows to avoid recognition.

He comes as a seeker of truth. But he comes at night.

He comes not in an official capacity but in a personal one. It is a chancy meeting. Gossip could hurt him. He has much to lose—his prestige as Israel's teacher, his position on the ruling council, his entire peer group.

But still he comes. Not for curiosity's sake but for conscience' sake.

The buying and selling in the temple courtyard has always bothered him. But he looked the other way. "What's good for business is good for the temple," the moneychangers would say, flashing their toothy smiles as he passed them on his way to the temple. But he always felt uneasy about it. Unclean.

Then this Jesus came. And he didn't like what he saw either. Something about the way he upended their tables and chased their animals from the courtyard seemed . . . seemed . . . like the cleansing wrath of God, burning away the dross that had accumulated around the temple.

But Jesus turned over more than the tables of the moneychangers that day. He upended the wooden thinking of the most prominent teacher in all Israel.

How the words of this unorthodox Jesus haunted Nicodemus: "How dare you turn my Father's house into a market!" . . . "Destroy this temple, and I will raise it again in three days."

Who could explain such words?

Israel asked its teacher. But the teacher had no explanation.

And the report of Jesus changing the water into wine. Who could explain that? How could Jesus do such a thing unless . . . unless God's hand was truly upon him. But he has no credentials, no formal schooling, and he shows no desire to be a part of the inner circle of religious leadership. He's an enigma, this Jesus.

Could he . . . ? No. And yet . . .

Night after night, Nicodemus wrestles with the same question: "Could this be the Messiah?" And night after sleepless night, it backs him into a corner, pressing him for an answer.

So he comes. At night, yes. But he comes.

No doubt, Jesus is exhausted from a day of teaching, answering questions, performing miracles. But he is accessible, always accessible, to the one who comes. And he meets Nicodemus when Nicodemus dares to meet him. At night.

It is a disarming meeting for this Pharisee, both theologically and personally. And as the conversation see-saws back and forth, the weight of it falling on Jesus, it's plain to see, even at night, who is the teacher and who is the one taking notes.

Nicodemus listens. Quietly. Respectfully. Intently. Peering deep into Jesus' eyes.

Nicodemus has rubbed shoulders with the most respected minds in the religious hierarchy. Some were his former teachers; some, his former students. They were the elite. He has peered into all of their eyes. And he always felt the same way, that something vital was missing, missing from all of their lives—including his.

Now as his soul is drawn into the eyes of Jesus, he senses he is touching the hem of a divine garment. The look in Jesus' eyes. The authority in his voice. Instead of jots and tittles of the law, he speaks words of life.

A lifetime of studying and teaching the Word, and now Nicodemus is face to face with the Word incarnate.

He came in darkness. Now he stands in the glowing presence of the Light of the World. He is a short step from the kingdom of God, at the very gate. And as the fluid words cascade from Jesus' lips, he realizes—this is he of whom the prophets spoke.

A spark touches the far edges of his soul, but it is a slow burn. For Nicodemus is a careful man. And he has much to lose.

Still, an ember has fallen into his heart. An ember that tragedy will someday fan to a blaze of courage. And it will be this tragedy that brings Nicodemus out of the shadows to the side of the Savior . . . in the full light of day.

PRAYER

earest Lord Jesus,

Thank you for being such a good teacher. For giving me simple illustrations of profound truths. Thank you for being so direct, for not skirting the hard questions. And thank you for answers, even though at times I am slow to grasp them.

Thank you for being such a willing teacher. Willing to go anywhere—to a Samaritan well or to a Damascus road. Willing to meet anyone—Pharisee or prostitute. Willing to go anytime—at noon or at night.

Thank you that I can come and bring my doubts, as did Thomas; my fears, as did Joseph of Arimathea; my shame, as did the woman caught in adultery; my questions, as did Nicodemus.

Thank you for the time you met with me at night, when you told me the bad news that I stood outside the gates of your kingdom. And the good news, that all I would have to do to enter would be to take a step of faith out of the darkness and into your light.

I confess, there are times when I have loved the darkness more than the light. Even as your child. And even now, there are times I walk along gray borders, flirting with the enticing shadows cast by the world. There have been times I have made this world not a brighter place but a darker one. By my thoughts. By my words. By my deeds. For all these shameful times I have been an unworthy subject, forgive me, I pray, O most worthy King.

Help me to walk in the light as you yourself are in the

light. Where there is darkness, let me be a beacon of light. And if not a beacon, a torch. And if not a torch, a candle. And if not a candle, then at least a spark to ignite others.

O Lord, may I never be ashamed of you or of being seen with you or of being associated with you in any way. "Sooner far, let evening blush to own a star. But may this my glory be, that you are not ashamed of me. . . ."

An
Intimate Moment
With a
Woman at a Well

ow he had to go through Samaria. So he came to a town in Samaria called Sychar, near the plot of ground Jacob had given to his son Joseph. Jacob's well was there, and Jesus, tired as he was from the journey, sat down by the well. It was about the sixth hour.

When a Samaritan woman came to draw water, Jesus said to her, "Will you give me a drink?" (His disciples had gone into the town to buy food.)

The Samaritan woman said to him, "You are a Jew and I am a Samaritan woman. How can you ask me for a drink?" (For Jews do not associate with Samaritans.)

Jesus answered her, "If you knew the gift of God and who it is that asks you for a drink, you would have asked him and he would have given you living water."

"Sir," the woman said, "you have nothing to draw with and the well is deep. Where can you get this living water? Are you greater than our father Jacob, who gave us the well and drank from it himself, as did also his sons and his flocks and herds?"

Jesus answered, "Everyone who drinks this water will be thirsty again, but whoever drinks the water I give him will never thirst. Indeed, the water I give him will become in him a spring of water welling up to eternal life."

The woman said to him, "Sir, give me this water so that I won't get thirsty and have to keep coming here to draw water."

He told her, "Go, call your husband and come back."

"I have no husband," she replied.

Jesus said to her, "You are right when you say you have no husband. The fact is, you have had five husbands, and the man you now have is not your husband. What you have just said is quite true."

"Sir," the woman said, "I can see that you are a prophet. Our fathers worshiped on this mountain, but you Jews claim that the place where we must worship is in Jerusalem."

Jesus declared, "Believe me, woman, a time is coming when you will worship the Father neither on this mountain nor in Jerusalem. You Samaritans worship what you do not know; we worship what we do know, for salvation is from the Jews. Yet a time is coming and has now come when the true worshipers will worship the Father in spirit and truth, for they are the kind of worshipers the Father seeks. God is spirit, and his worshipers must worship in spirit and in truth."

The woman said, "I know that Messiah" (called Christ) "is coming. When he comes, he will explain everything to us."

Then Jesus declared, "I who speak to you am he."

Just then his disciples returned and were surprised to find him talking with a woman. But no one asked, "What do you want?" or "Why are you talking with her?"

Then, leaving her water jar, the woman went back to the town and said to the people, "Come, see a man who told me everything I ever did. Could this be the Christ?"

They came out of the town and made their way toward him. . . .

Many of the Samaritans from that town believed in him because of the woman's testimony, "He told me everything I ever did." So when the Samaritans came to him, they urged him to stay with them, and he stayed two days. And because of his words many more became believers.

They said to the woman, "We no longer believe just because of what you said; now we have heard for ourselves, and we know that this man really is the Savior of the world."

John 4:4–30, 39–42

MEDITATION

The Palestinian sun glares its impartial eye upon both this nameless Samaritan woman and upon the Savior of the world. Weary from travel, he stops to rest beside Jacob's well. She, too, is on her way to that well, keeping (unknown to her) an appointment with destiny. For *she* is the reason "he had to go through Samaria."

Through sheer curtains of undulating heat she comes. She too is weary. Not so much from the water jar she carries on her head as from the emptiness she carries in her heart. The husked emptiness left over from the wild oats of years past.

The torrents of passion, once swift in her life, have now run their course. She is weathered and worn, her face eroded by the gulleys of a spent life.

That she comes at noon, the hottest hour of the day, whispers a rumor of her reputation. The other women come at dawn, a cooler, more comfortable hour. They come not only to draw water but to take off their veils and slip out from under the thumb of a male-dominated society. They come for companionship, to talk, to laugh, and to barter gossip—much of which centers around this woman. So, shunned by Sychar's wives, she braves the sun's scorn. Anything to avoid the searing stares of the more reputable.

For a span of five husbands she has come to this well. Always at noon. Always alone.

Accusing thoughts are her only companions as she ponders the futile road her life has traveled. She thinks back to the crossroads in her life, of roads that might have been taken, of happiness that might have been found. But she knows she can never go back.

She's at a dead end right now, living with a man in a relationship that leads nowhere. She knows that. But for now she needs him. His presence fills the lonely nights with a measured cup of companionship, however shallow or tepid.

She has gone from man to man like one lost in the desert, sun-struck and delirious. For her, marriage has been a retreating mirage. Again and again she has returned to the matrimonial well, hoping to draw from it something to quench her thirst for love and happiness. But again and again she has left that well disappointed.

And so, under the weight of such thoughts she comes to Jacob's well, her empty water jar a telling symbol of her life.

As her eyes meet the Savior's, he sees within her a cavernous aching, a cistern in her soul that will forever remain empty unless he fills it. Through her eyes, he peers into her past with tenderness. He sees every burst of passion's flame . . . and every passion's burnt out failure.

Yet to her, an anonymous woman with a failed life, he gives the most profound discourse in Scripture on the subject of worship—that God is spirit and that worship is not an approach of the body to a church, but an approach of the soul to the spirit of God. A cutting revelation to one who has lived so much of her life in the realm of the physical rather than the spiritual.

But equally remarkable is what Jesus doesn't say. He states her past and present marital status but makes no reference to her sin. He gives no call to repent. He presents no structured plan of salvation. He offers no prayer.

What he does do is take her away from the city and bring her to a quiet well. There he shows her a reflection of herself. Understandably, she shrinks back.

She then takes a detour down the backroads of theology. But with the words "I who speak to you am he," Jesus brings her back to face the giver and his remarkable gift—living water. Not a wage to be earned. Not a prize to be won. But a gift to be received.

To her this stranger was first simply "a Jew" . . . then "Sir" . . . then "a prophet." Now she sees him for who he really is—"Messiah."

In that intimate moment of perception, she leaves to tell this good news to the city that has both shared her and shunned her. Behind, left in the sand, is her empty water jar. Stretching before her is a whole new life. And with her heart overflowing with living water she starts to run. Slowly at first. Then as fast as her new legs will take her.

PRAYER

ear Lord,

Even though I have the same living water within me that you gave the Samaritan woman, so often I find myself searching for other things to fill my life.

It's inconceivable that anyone who's tasted of your goodness would drink from any other well. Yet I have. Money. Success. Pleasure. Popularity. Security. In the end, all dry wells.

But how many times have I lowered my cup into their depths? And how many times have I brought it up empty?

Keep vivid in my mind the time when you met me by the well and said, "I who speak to you am he." And may the memory of that sacred moment keep me from wandering to seek water at any other well than yours.

Grant me diligence in watching over that sacred well. And let me not forget that even living water can be stagnated by indifference or tainted by the impurities I tolerate in my life.

Keep my faith pure so it will be a deep well where others can come to be refreshed. And as they do, O Lord Jesus, I pray that you would meet them there . . . as you did that Samaritan woman . . . as you did me . . . and give them living water.

Renew in me, O Savior, a zeal like this Samaritan woman had—a zeal to tell her friends, her acquaintances, and even strangers about you. Not a zeal to worship in this church or that. Not a zeal for theology. Not a zeal for causes. But a zeal for you. For you and only you. . . .

AN
INTIMATE MOMENT
WITH
PETER

SCRIPTURE

One day as Jesus was standing by the Lake of Gennesaret, with the people crowding around him and listening to the word of God, he saw at the water's edge two boats, left there by the fishermen, who were washing their nets. He got into one of the boats, the one belonging to Simon, and asked him to put out a little from shore. Then he sat down and taught the people from the boat.

When he had finished speaking, he said to Simon, "Put out into deep water, and let down the nets for a catch."

Simon answered, "Master, we've worked hard all night and haven't caught anything. But because you say so, I will let down the nets."

When they had done so, they caught such a large number of fish that their nets began to break. So they signaled their partners in the other boat to come and help them, and they came and filled both boats so full that they began to sink.

When Simon Peter saw this, he fell at Jesus' knees and said, "Go away from me, Lord; I am a sinful man!" For he and all his companions were astonished at the catch of fish they had taken, and so were James and John, the sons of Zebedee, Simon's partners.

Then Jesus said to Simon, "Don't be afraid; from now on you will catch men." So they pulled their boats up on shore, left everything and followed him.

Luke 5:1–11

28

MEDITATION

The crowd clamors to get first pick of the fishermen's catch. But the sea was a miser that night. And the boats returned empty.

Jesus is among the crowd that morning and seizes the opportunity to teach. His teaching of the Word is so different from the scribes and Pharisees. He doesn't hold it over their heads like a club. He simply holds it up to the light. And thus held, a rainbow of color washes hope over the gray crowd. Colors of a new kingdom in the first blush of its dawn.

Peter is one of the fishermen who returned from the sea that morning with nothing to show for it but a sore back and nets that needed cleaning. Over those nets he now hunches, prying loose the slender, silky fingers of seaweed. As he does, the ascending sun warms his chilled shoulders.

His brother Andrew is the one who first brought Peter to Jesus. He told him what John the Baptist said about Jesus being the Lamb of God. And he told him Jesus was the Messiah. Peter followed Jesus around Capernaum as he taught in the synagogues and on the seashores. Like a Mediterranean sponge, he soaked in everything he heard. Which is what he's doing now as, square by square, he goes through the mindless routine of washing his net.

The eager crowd edges closer until there is no margin of shore left where Jesus can stand. So he gets into Peter's boat and asks him to push out. Quick to do the Master's bidding, the big fisherman oars out a short distance and drops anchor.

Behind them the sun glints off the scalloped water in little flashes of gold, paving a shimmering road from boat to shore. And over that road the words of Jesus travel to the crowd once again.

With Jesus in the bow Peter sits in the middle of the boat, taking a mental knife to every sentence, just as he would to get at the fresh white meat of a fish.

Finally Jesus finishes with the crowd—but not with Peter. As if he is now the captain of Peter's boat, he issues an order, "Put out into deep water, and let down the nets for a catch."

The burly fisherman picks his words carefully so as not to offend. "Master," he begins, little knowing how far or how deep this master's domain extends. "We've worked hard all night and haven't caught anything."

To himself he thinks, *Lord, no offense, but this is my profession. Every fisherman knows that if you're going to catch fish, it's going to be at night when they rise from the depths to feed on the surface. And every fisherman knows that when the sun comes up, it drives them down below the reach of the nets.*

But Peter's respect for Jesus conceals these thoughts. And out of respect he obeys: "But because you say so, I will let down the nets."

As the hired hands row to the deep water, Peter feels a little foolish. But he says nothing. Nor does Jesus until he calls out, "Stop. Here. This is a good spot."

The men take the weighted nets and heave them unfurling into the sea. As the nets sink, the silence continues.

Peter holds the rope next to Jesus. This is an embarrassing moment for the experienced fisherman. And he is careful not to look at Jesus or his men. He just peers out to the sea.

But at the far end is a tug. Then another. And another. Suddenly, the nets are alive and jumping in their hands. The surface churns with fish slapping the sea and flashing in the sun. The fishermen strain at the ropes, and a few of the twined squares snap.

"James! John!" Peter calls out to his partners. "Come quick. We've got a catch so big the nets are breaking! Hurry!"

Above them hover squawking flurries of herons, cranes, and cormorants, waiting to dart in and steal away what they can of the catch.

And all the while the nets pull the men's arms. The sockets of their shoulders burn as ligaments and tendons are stretched to the limit. The ropes cut into their hands. And their muscles twist to wring sweat from every pore. Their words are choppy: "Careful . . . come my way . . . that's it . . . steady . . . cut some slack."

When the other boat arrives, the fishermen team up to pour the bulging net of silver into their empty hulls. But the treasure is so great that the portside rim dips below the waterline, spilling the sea into their boat. The men bail feverishly and start throwing fish back. All the men, that is, except Peter.

A jagged revelation rips through his soul and stops him

31

in his tracks, *This is no human Messiah; this Master's dominion reaches even to the depths of the sea.*

He whirls around to look at Jesus, and their eyes lock. Suddenly the murky depths of Peter's heart are dredged to the surface. And he realizes how unworthy he is even to be in the same boat with Jesus.

Trembling, he sloshes over to Jesus and falls at his knees, "Go away from me, Lord; I am a sinful man!"

An overwhelming sense of awe shivers through the crew as they await the Master's response.

But his words carry no thunder. They are calm and full of promise. "Don't be afraid; from now on you will catch men."

When they finally reach the shore, Peter's career as a fisherman is over. He leaves behind a business with a steady income, a business with assets, a business with a future. Without once looking back. Without once taking inventory of his losses.

What he gives up are boats, nets, and fish. What he gains is Jesus. And that proved to be the best business decision of his life.

PRAYER

ear Master,

Help me to be faithful in little things like cleaning nets, knowing that they could be your way of preparing me for greater things—like fishing for men.

Help me to obey simply and solely "because you say so." And keep me from thinking that since I have fished a few waters that somehow I know better than you the course my life should take and the place my nets should be dropped.

Call me, Lord, out from a shallow faith near the shore, which requires no risks and offers no rewards. Call me to a deeper commitment to you.

And when you call, grant that I would be quick in my boat, swift to my oars, and fast with my nets. And I pray, grant me the eyes to see who it is who labors by my side—an awesome and almighty God.

Take me to a place where I have worked hard by my own strength and yet ended up with empty nets. Take me there to show me the depths of your dominion and the net-breaking fullness of your power.

Keep me ever aware that you are Lord. And ever aware that I am a sinful person. And in that knowledge keep me ever on my knees before you.

At your bidding, O Master, I will let down my nets. And at your bidding I will leave them forever behind. For what you have to offer is infinitely more than all the seas of this world ever could. . . .

AN
INTIMATE MOMENT
WITH A
POSSESSED MAN

SCRIPTURE

They went across the lake to the region of the Gerasenes. When Jesus got out of the boat, a man with an evil spirit came from the tombs to meet him. This man lived in the tombs, and no one could bind him any more, not even with a chain. For he had often been chained hand and foot, but he tore the chains apart and broke the irons on his feet. No one was strong enough to subdue him. Night and day among the tombs and in the hills he would cry out and cut himself with stones.

When he saw Jesus from a distance, he ran and fell on his knees in front of him. He shouted at the top of his voice, "What do you want with me, Jesus, Son of the Most High God? Swear to God that you won't torture me!" For Jesus had said to him, "Come out of this man, you evil spirit!"

Then Jesus asked him, "What is your name?"

"My name is Legion," he replied, "for we are many." And he begged Jesus again and again not to send them out of the area.

A large herd of pigs was feeding on the nearby hillside. The demons begged Jesus, "Send us among the pigs; allow us to go into them." He gave them permission, and the evil spirits came out and went into the pigs. The herd, about two thousand in number, rushed down the steep bank into the lake and were drowned.

Those tending the pigs ran off and reported this in the town and countryside, and the people went out to see what had happened. When they came to Jesus, they saw the man who had been possessed by the legion of demons, sitting there, dressed and in his right mind; and they were afraid. Those who had seen it told the people what had happened to the demon-possessed man—and told about the pigs as well. Then the people began to plead with Jesus to leave their region.

As Jesus was getting into the boat, the man who had been demon-possessed begged to go with him. Jesus did not let him, but said, "Go home to your family and tell them how much the Lord has done for you, and how he has had mercy on you." So the man went away and began to tell in the Decapolis how much Jesus had done for him. And all the people were amazed.

Mark 5:1–20

MEDITATION

He is a creature you would probably meet only in your worst nightmares, if even there. He is a man possessed with demons. They drive him to violence. They drive him to cry out like a wild dog howling in the night. They drive him to the solitary places—in the hills, among the tombs.

There he froths about like a rabid animal, living on the ragged, outer fringe of humanity. Luke tells us it's been a long time since he's worn clothes or lived in a house.

There are no houses in Palestine for men like him. No hospitals. No asylums. Like jackals they are left to roam this no-man's land on the eastern shore of the Sea of Galilee. Their only refuge is the holes hewn in the hillside to bury the dead.

His hair is a matted tangle of filth. His body is scarred white around his wrists and ankles where manacles once tried to restrain him. His haggard body is gashed with the self-inflicted punishment of stones. Barely a vestige of humanity remains.

How did this image of God become so marred and defaced? How did he get to where he is now? How did he end up here—his only home, a tomb; his only companions, demons?

Was he not once some mother's little boy? Was he not once a child who played "make believe" and made mud pies and skipped through the streets? And yet now, now his life has fallen into an abyss where there is no memory of the past and no hope for the future—only the torture of the present, a nightmare of unfettered terror.

Somehow, somewhere, in some time past, the forces of darkness gained a foothold in his life. How, we are not told. Or where. Or when. But some time ago, they sought him out like a pride of lions seeking prey. Somewhere he gave ground. Somehow he gave them an opening through which to attack. And he's been a prisoner ever since.

Now his body is a beachhead for Satan. And it is onto this beachhead that Jesus now lands.

As they reach the shore, the disciples are still scratching their heads. They have just witnessed the most remarkable demonstration of sheer, unbridled power they have ever seen—Jesus calming the storm. With his words— "Quiet! Be still!"—he not only calmed the wind but instantaneously stilled the waves by calming the undercurrents that kept them in motion. Little do the disciples realize that they are traveling headlong into yet another storm.

His fledgling students have just learned that Jesus is Lord over the natural realm. In this sequel to that lesson, they will learn that he is also Lord over the supernatural realm. And they will observe firsthand that he can calm a tormented soul as easily as he calmed a tempestuous sea.

The disciples pull their boat onto the dry beach in a region of tombs and pigs, both unclean for the Jew. The mood is ominous and foreboding.

In front of them steep limestone cliffs jut skyward. But their eyes are not on the dramatic scenery. From one of the caverned tombs storms a wild man, ranting and raving as he rushes toward them in windblown fury.

Like a warm front hitting a cold front head on, the forces of good and evil collide. Infinite good versus incorrigible evil.

The disciples step back to brace themselves for the stormy encounter. But Jesus courageously stands his ground. And before this forceful gale crashes against them, Jesus calls out, "Come out of this man, you evil spirit!"

Immediately the violent gust abates. The wild man throws himself at Jesus' feet. The Greeks did this before their deified rulers. Slaves did it before their masters. And the demons now do it with fear and trembling in his presence.

His scream echoes off the stone cliffs, "What do you want with me, Jesus, Son of the Most High God?"

There is no confusion about who Jesus is. The religious leaders may debate. The crowds may be divided. But for the forces of evil his identity cannot be denied.

With the question "What is your name?", Jesus lifts the veil on the dark face of the underworld.

The throaty voice rasps its reply, "My name is Legion, for we are many."

A Roman legion is six thousand. How many are in this legion we aren't told. But the regiment of evil is formidable. Even so, these diabolical forces cower at the feet of Christ. They grovel in the sand, begging not to be sent to the Abyss of eternal punishment. They plea instead for a lesser punishment—banishment into a herd of pigs.

Jesus grants the request. And the two thousand pigs feeding on the grassy plateau become host to these wicked parasites. In a crazed frenzy the pigs rush to hurl themselves off the cliffs into the wet jaws of the waiting sea.

Meanwhile, the pig herders rush off in the opposite direction, reporting the bizarre event to the townspeople. When they return and see the released man, they become afraid, not of the demons, but of the deliverer. And as intensely as the demons pleaded to go into the pigs, the townspeople plead for Jesus to go.

What a tragedy. Jesus is at their very shore to cast out demons, to heal the sick, to tell the good news of his kingdom, to bring a blessing. And they beg him to leave.

How many lives went unchanged, how many sick went unhealed, how many captives went unreleased because a herd of swine was judged as more valuable than a human soul?

Jesus never stays where he's not welcome. He gets into the boat to leave. But now another man pleads with him, the man who had been possessed. He begs to go with Jesus, to follow him, to tell of the great things the Savior has done for him.

But Jesus does a strange thing. He tells him no. The man can't understand. Even the disciples are shocked at the refusal. Dedicated followers are so hard to find. And yet this man is refused the opportunity.

No, this man is to go home, to run behind the lines. And run he will. He will start at home. Then he will tell the entire city. And then all the ten Gentile cities of the Decapolis.

Life for this man changed when a storm blew Jesus his way. On that tattered shore Jesus reached into the most terrifying of tombs. To pull a naked prisoner from the darkness. To set him free. To dress him in his right mind. And, to send him home. So that a lost little boy could be reunited with his mom. So he could skip in the streets once more. And so he could tell, with childlike glee, the great things the Lord did for him.

PRAYER

ear Master who rules
with such a calm hand,

I pray that you would give me eyes to see that the true
battle is spiritual not physical.

> For our struggle is not against flesh and blood,
> but against the rulers, against the authorities,
> against the powers of this dark world and
> against the spiritual forces of evil in the
> heavenly realms.

Help me to realize that no matter how violent their
opposition, people are not the enemy. They are prisoners
of the enemy. Help me to realize that you died to free
those prisoners. And in that knowledge give me the courage, I pray, to penetrate their shores so they might be
brought out of their tombs, delivered of their demons,
dressed in their right mind, and given the privilege to sit
at your feet.

Help me to boldly take a beachhead of Satan for the
kingdom of God. To banish his forces. And to be brave in
the knowledge that though they are legion, you are Lord.

Help me to realize that the true battleground is the
human heart. It is over this territory that the forces of
good and evil draw their swords.

Knowing that, Lord, on this day, this hour, I surrender
my heart to you—my hopes, my fears, my dreams, my de-
sires, my ambitions, my anxieties, my love, and my loyalty.

May it be one more victory for the kingdom of God.
And one less battle you have to fight. . . .

An
INTIMATE MOMENT
WITH A
HEMORRHAGING WOMAN

SCRIPTURE

A large crowd followed and pressed around him. And a woman was there who had been subject to bleeding for twelve years. She had suffered a great deal under the care of many doctors and had spent all she had, yet instead of getting better she grew worse. When she heard about Jesus, she came up behind him in the crowd and touched his cloak, because she thought, "If I just touch his clothes, I will be healed." Immediately her bleeding stopped and she felt in her body that she was freed from her suffering.

At once Jesus realized that power had gone out from him. He turned around in the crowd and asked, "Who touched my clothes?"

"You see the people crowding against you," his disciples answered, "and yet you can ask, 'Who touched me?' "

But Jesus kept looking around to see who had done it. Then the woman, knowing what had happened to her, came and fell at his feet and, trembling with fear, told him the whole truth. He said to her, "Daughter, your faith has healed you. Go in peace and be freed from your suffering."

Mark 5:24–34

MEDITATION

God only knows how much she's suffered. She has lived with a bleeding uterus for twelve humiliating years. She has been labeled unclean by the rabbis and subjected to the Levitical prohibitions: unable to touch others or to be touched. Ostracized by the synagogue. Orphaned by society.

And orphaned also by God, or so she thinks. She has prayed. She has pleaded. But for twelve agonizing years God has been silent.

During that time, she was put out of the city's back door and shoved down its steps. Ever since, she has foraged in the side streets and alleyways for some scant leftovers of hope.

Her eyes are downcast as you pass by. She is self-conscious . . . ashamed . . . and afraid. She fears the condescension in your eyes. She fears the indifference of your shoulder turned coldly against her. But most of all, she fears the gavel you bring down on her life. She fears the rapped judgment that her illness is the direct result of some personal sin. And with a bleeding uterus, anyone could guess what kind of sin she has committed. "Sexual, no doubt," are the whispered innuendos. "Some perversion, most likely," are the gossiped indictments.

And so, besides the shame of the constant bleeding, she bears the burden of its stigma. She carries this weight everywhere she goes. Trudging from doctor to doctor, she has tried to find a place to lay her burden down. The doctors have filled her mind with hopes and her body with folk remedies, but in the end, the only thing they relieved her of was her money.

She is destitute now. And being out of money, the doctors finally admit there is nothing they can do for her. Her life is ebbing away. The steady loss of blood over the years has taken its toll. She is anemic, pale, and tired. So very, very tired.

She is tired of the shame. Tired of the stigma. Tired of the charlatans.

God only knows how much she's suffered.

Every illusion she had about life is shattered. Suffering has a way of doing that. And swept away with those illusions are her dreams. Suffering has a way of doing that, too.

She no longer dreams of marriage and a family . . . of combing the hair of a daughter or wiping the dirty face of a son . . . of bouncing a grandbaby on her knee . . . of being taken care of in her old age by loved ones . . . of golden memories she can treasure. Her suffering has whisked those dreams into little broken piles.

But stories of another physician reach down to pick up the pieces of those dreams. A physician who charges no fee. A physician who asks for nothing in return. Who has no hidden agenda beyond making a sick world well again.

She has heard of this physician, this Jesus who comes not to the healthy but to the sick. Who comes not to the strong but to the downtrodden. Who comes not to those with well-ordered lives but to those whose lives are filled with physical and moral chaos.

And she has heard of Jesus' success among incurables: the curing of an uncontrollable demoniac . . . the raising of a widow's dead son . . . the healing of a leper.

A leper, she thinks. Another untouchable. Another orphan taken by the scruff of the neck and thrown from society's back door. The divine physician simply touched this disease-eaten man and he became clean and whole. *Certainly,* she thinks, *if I can find this Jesus and but touch the fringe of his garment, I too will be cleansed and made whole.*

And so, with that thin thread of faith, this frail needle of a woman stitches her way through the crowd.

Her tired frame is jostled by those clustered around Jesus. They are pressing him, brushing shoulders, and rubbing against him—the curious, the eager, and the desperate.

This desperate woman pushes her empty hand through a broken seam in the crowd and, for a fleeting moment, clutches the corner of his garment. Jesus is pulled back. Not by the grasp of her hands so much as by the grasp of her faith. Power leaves him to surge through the hemorrhaging woman, and immediately she feels the rush of her youthful health returning. In the flood of those feelings, she releases her grasp and is swept away by the crowd.

But Jesus doesn't let her get away. Although the crowd was pressing in on him, her touch was different. And that touch stopped him in his tracks. How ready Jesus is to respond to the hand of outstretched faith.

In obedience to his summons she comes—trembling, flushed with embarrassment, fearful. But she comes. And between the lines of her confession, punctuated haltingly by her tears, Jesus reads the whole sad story of the last twelve years.

He sees the isolation. He sees the introspection. He sees the insecurity.

God only knows how much she's suffered.

The crowd blurs in the watery edges of her eyes. For an intimate moment she sees only Jesus. And he sees only her. Face to face, physician and patient.

And with the tender word "Daughter," he gives this orphan a new home within the family of God. He gives her healing. And he gives her back her dreams.

PRAYER

ear Most Merciful of Physicians,

Help me to realize that it was not the healthy who reached out to you. They bunched up in crowds, but it was those who suffered greatly who reached out to grasp you.

It was the people in the streets, not in the sitting rooms of society, that groped for your garment. It was needy people. People with outstretched arms. People with empty hands. People who had nothing to offer but the faith that you could make them whole.

I confess, O Lord, how often I have followed in the crowd pressed around you. Yet how few times have those brushes with you changed my life. I have touched you, but only in the rush hour of religious activity.

Sunday after Sunday I take my part in the crowd as I sit through the service. I repeat the liturgy, sing the hymns, hear the sermon. I read my Bible, say my prayers, give my money. I attend the right seminars, tune in the right programs, read the right books.

How could I be so close to your presence yet so far from your power?

Could it be that my arms are folded? Could it be that my hands are full?

I pray that if my arms are complacent, you would unfold them in outstretched longing for you. And if my hands are full, I pray that you would empty them so that I might cling only to you.

Help me to understand, Lord Jesus, that the hemorrhaging woman's faith was forged on the anvil of twelve long years of suffering. Years of disillusionment. Years of shattered dreams.

Thank you, Lord Jesus, for seeing every hemorrhage in my life through merciful eyes, eyes that understand, eyes that see the whole story of my life.

Thank you for your willingness to staunch my suffering. And thank you that I can lay my troubles at your feet and go my way in peace. . . .

An
INTIMATE MOMENT
WITH A
WOMAN CAUGHT IN ADULTERY

SCRIPTURE

Jesus went to the Mount of Olives. At dawn he appeared again in the temple courts, where all the people gathered around him, and he sat down to teach them. The teachers of the law and the Pharisees brought in a woman caught in adultery. They made her stand before the group and said to Jesus, "Teacher, this woman was caught in the act of adultery. In the Law Moses commanded us to stone such women. Now what do you say?" They were using this question as a trap, in order to have a basis for accusing him.

But Jesus bent down and started to write on the ground with his finger. When they kept on questioning him, he straightened up and said to them, "If any one of you is without sin, let him be the first to throw a stone at her." Again he stooped down and wrote on the ground.

At this, those who heard began to go away one at a time, the older ones first, until only Jesus was left, with the woman still standing there. Jesus straightened up and asked her, "Woman, where are they? Has no one condemned you?"

"No one, sir," she said.

"Then neither do I condemn you," Jesus declared. "Go now and leave your life of sin."

John 8:1–11

MEDITATION

The ruckus can be heard a block away, interrupting the peaceful yawn of the city. And into the midst of the crowd that has gathered to hear Jesus teach, she is thrown.

Barefoot and disheveled. Sweaty from the struggle, she stands there, a mop of hair hanging in her face. Her jaw is fixed. Her teeth clenched. Her lips pressed into thin lines of resistance. Her nostrils flared in breathy defiance.

"Adulteress!" they charge. "Caught in the act!"

But caught by whom? And why?

The teachers and Pharisees appeal to the Law and call for the death penalty. But for a person to be put to death the Law requires that there be at least two eyewitnesses. Eyewitnesses to the very act of adultery.

Can you picture the scene? Peeping Pharisees nosing around her windowsill. How long did they watch? How much did they see? And were not their hearts filled with adultery when they eavesdropped on that clandestine rendezvous? At least two witnessed the act. Yet without compunction for the sin. Or compassion for the sinner.

When they had seen enough, these guardians of morality stormed the door to the bedroom where she lay naked and defenseless. She struggled as they wrestled to subdue her. They pushed her into her clothes like a pig into a gunny sack to be taken, kicking and squealing, to market.

Thus she arrives at the temple. Torn from the privacy of a stolen embrace and thrust into public shame.

This is it, she tells herself, *this is the end.* Her fate forever at the hands of men. From their hands she has received bread. Now it is to be stones.

And so she stands there, sullen, her eyes deep sinkholes of hate. And every eye that circles her returns the searing hate, branding a scarlet letter onto her soul. Every eye, that is, except for the eyes of Jesus.

Meanwhile, where is her lover? By prior agreement allowed to slip through a window? Part of the plot, no doubt—the plot to ensnare Jesus. For it is not the woman they want to bring down or the Law to uphold. It is Jesus they want. She is only the bait; and their question, the spring to the trap.

Time and again Jesus has shown compassion on sinners. And yet the Law of Moses is uncompromising and impartial in its treatment of them. If the religious leaders can somehow wedge Jesus between his loyalty to the stone tablets of the Law and his steadfast love for sinners, certainly that would squeeze out his true colors for all to see. If he frees her, they reason, as he most certainly will, he forsakes the Law. Then they will have cause to accuse him before the Sanhedrin.

The question they use to spring the trap is not a theoretical one like, "whose wife will she be in the resurrection?" It is a question of life and death in whose balance hangs not only the fate of this woman but the fate of Christ as well.

Disappointingly for the leaders, he doesn't enter into a debate. He simply stoops down to gather his thoughts.

The silence is deafening; the drama, intense. With his finger he writes in the sand. The necks of the righteous crane to decipher the writing. What he writes will forever remain a mystery. Maybe it is the sins the crowd has committed. Maybe it is a quote from Moses. Maybe it is the names of the prominent leaders there. Whatever he writes is for their eyes, not ours.

Jesus stands up. All eyes are fixed on him.

At last he responds, "If any one of you is without sin, let him be the first to throw a stone at her."

One by one the stones thud to the ground. And one by one the men leave. Starting with the oldest, perhaps because they are the wisest—or the most guilty.

Jesus stoops to write again. This time it is only for her eyes.

They are alone now—lawbreaker and lawgiver. And the only one qualified to condemn her, doesn't.

She takes a deep breath. Her heart is a fluttering moth held captive in his hands.

The Savior has stood up for this unknown woman and fought for her. She is his victory. He stands up again, this time to free her.

"Has no one condemned you?" he asks.

Timid words stumble from her lips, "No one, sir."

She waits for a reply. Certainly a sermon must be gathering momentum in the wings. But no sermon comes.

57

What comes are words of grace, "Neither do I condemn you," and words of truth, that her life of sin needs to be left behind.

The trembling subsides. Her face softens. The furrows on her forehead relax.

Should I stay? Should I ask a question? Should I thank him? The questions race through her mind.

She looks into his face. His forehead relaxes. It has been an ordeal for him, too. He takes a breath and his smile seems to say "Go, you're free now."

She opens her mouth to say something. But the words don't come. She walks away, and before she turns the corner, she stops . . . pauses . . . and looks back to thank him. But Jesus is seated, his face in his hands, praying to the Father. And she turns to go her way, leaving behind her a life of sin.

There are no tears as she leaves. Years later there will be. At odd moments during the day: when she looks at her children asleep in their beds; when she waves good-bye to her husband as he walks to work in the morning; when she kneads bread in the solitude of her kitchen.

A marriage she never would have had . . . a family she never would have had . . . a life she never would have had—were it not for such a wonderful savior. A savior who stood up for her when others wanted to stone her. A Savior who stooped to pick her up and send her on her way, forgiven.

PRAYER

ear Lord Jesus,

I confess with shame that there are times I have stood in the midst, condemned. And there are times I have stood in the crowd, condemning.

There are times my heart has been filled with adultery. And there are times my hands have been filled with stones.

Forgive me for a heart that is so prone to wander, so quick to forget my vows to you. Forgive me, too, for my eagerness in bringing you the sins of others. And my reluctance in bringing you my own. Forgive me for the times I have stood smugly Pharisaic and measured out judgment to others. Others I am not qualified to judge. Others, who you, though qualified, refuse to.

Help me to be more like you, Jesus—full of grace and truth. Help me to live not by Law but by grace, by the spirit of compassion you showed to that woman so many mornings ago.

Give me, I pray, the pierced conscience of the older ones in regard to the stumblings of others so my hands may be first to drop their stones, and my feet, first to leave the circle of the self-righteous.

Thank you for those sweet words of forgiveness: "Neither do I condemn you." Words that flow so freely from your lips. Words that I have heard so often when I have stumbled. And in the strength of those unmerited words, help me to go my way and sin no more. . . .

". . . but only one thing

is needed."

AN
INTIMATE MOMENT
WITH
MARY AND MARTHA

SCRIPTURE

As Jesus and his disciples were on their way, he came to a village where a woman named Martha opened her home to him. She had a sister called Mary, who sat at the Lord's feet listening to what he said. But Martha was distracted by all the preparations that had to be made. She came to him and asked, "Lord, don't you care that my sister has left me to do the work by myself? Tell her to help me!"

"Martha, Martha," the Lord answered, "you are worried and upset about many things, but only one thing is needed. Mary has chosen what is better, and it will not be taken away from her."

Luke 10:38–42

MEDITATION

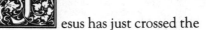

esus has just crossed the barren and unreceptive desert of Samaria and has resolutely set his face toward Jerusalem.

It is autumn, and the leaves collecting in little wind-blown drifts rustle to warn that winter is not far off. It will be the last winter for Jesus. In six months he will be dead. He knows that. So for him winter is already here, piercing his heart.

He stops two miles short of Jerusalem at a village on the eastern slope of the Mount of Olives. The village is Bethany.

There he comes seeking a shelter from the cold reality that awaits him in Jerusalem. He comes seeking a refuge from those biting winds. He comes seeking warmth.

And where he comes is to the home of Mary and Martha. Home is something unfamiliar to him. Underneath an olive tree on the side of a hill . . . by a fire on the seashore . . . in the hull of a fishing boat. These were just a few of his homes the past three years. For although foxes have holes and birds have nests, the Son of Man has nowhere to lay his head.

Laying his head to rest in a home is a rare treat for Jesus. Especially a home such as this—a home where he is recognized as Lord; a home where he is loved. And though the world receives him not, when he knocks at the door to this home, he is welcomed with open arms.

Martha, the older sister and owner of the house, is first to answer. Her excitement echoes through the house,

"Mary! Mary! Come quick! It's Jesus!" Mary darts to the door to greet him.

Immediately they tend to his needs. Martha brings him a drink of fresh water. Martha, so eager to serve. Energetic. First to roll up her sleeves and pitch in to help. Last to leave until every dish is cleaned and put away. Up early. First at the market. Haggles to get the best prices. To the point, sometimes even abrupt. The yokes of the eggs she serves for breakfast are never broken. The fruit she sets out in a wooden bowl on the table is always fresh and sweet. Dinner is never overcooked. The perfect hostess.

And Mary? Well, she's up about thirty minutes later. Sometimes goes with her sister to the market, but more often than not, doesn't. The haggling bothers her. Likes to cook, but doesn't like to clean up the mess. Perceptive. Asks few but thoughtful questions. Is a good listener. Sensitive and calm.

While Mary takes Jesus' sandals and washes his weary feet, Martha busies herself in the kitchen. Both are intently listening to him speak about the disciples. Of them going from village to village. Of them proclaiming the kingdom. Of them casting out demons. Of them healing the sick.

As Mary finishes her duties, she lays aside the basin of water and the washrag. She resumes sitting at his feet. The three times you see Mary in Scripture that is where she is, at the Savior's feet—on the occasion of this visit, at the death of her brother, and when she anoints his feet with perfume shortly before his death. Her physical posture reflects the posture of her heart. Humble. Reverent. Teachable. All the qualities of a good disciple. And there she sits, drinking in every word that pours so sweetly from his lips.

But torn between the conversation and her preparations, Martha's attention is drawn to the kitchen. Here she readies her feast. Nothing like a hot meal for a weary traveler. And nothing but the best for Jesus.

In her zeal to give the very best to Jesus she empties her cupboards, brings out the foods reserved for special occasions, and gets flour to make fresh bread.

Something eternal is in the making. But not in the kitchen. What's cooking in the kitchen will be gone in a meal. It is what's being prepared in the other room that will go on forever.

In the other room conversation takes a jog toward Samaria. The news isn't good. He wasn't welcome there because he is a Jew, and doors to entire villages were shut in his face. Throughout Galilee and Judea, opposition is also mounting. The religious community, so zealous to guard the rigid wineskins of its tradition, has decided it doesn't want the new wine he's offering. Jesus is a marked man. The hourglass has been turned on his life. And each day a little more sand funnels through. His hour is fast approaching.

The words enter Mary's heart like a dagger. But she does not resist the blade. She sits, quietly sheathing his words.

As Mary takes all this in, Martha is getting caught up in a whirlwind of activity in the kitchen. In the flurry she hears less and less of the conversation in the other room. Hers is a magnanimous gesture but a mistaken one. Because Jesus doesn't want food; he wants fellowship.

But Martha doesn't know that. Her hands work the dough vigorously as a broken necklace of sweat forms under her chin and separate beads glisten on her forehead. She wipes them away with the back of her hand and blows away a drip bulging from the tip of her nose.

As she works the dough, she thinks of everything else that needs to be done. All she hears now is the sound of the voices, not the words. And the sound grates against her.

I can't believe Mary isn't in here helping, she thinks. Martha pushes a fist into the dough. *She should be in here.* Another fist into the dough. *We could get this done in half the time.* She pulls and mashes, pulls and mashes. *You know, I'd like to hear what he has to say, too, but somebody's got to fix dinner.* Martha reaches for some flour and flings it on the lump. *They could at least come in here while they talk.* She works the flour into the expanding loaf. *I can't believe he just lets her sit there.* Another fist into the dough. *Here I am in the kitchen, sweating, working my fingers to the bone . . . doesn't he care?*

Finally, she's had enough. Martha throws down the dough and stomps into the living room. "Lord, don't you care that my sister has left me to do the work by myself? Tell her to help me!"

Martha is hot. She doesn't address Mary directly. She's

too mad. She doesn't even call her by name. She refers to her as "my sister." And in unsheathing her tongue, she reveals her anger, anger that is double-edged. The one side cuts Jesus, accusing him of lacking concern. The other cuts Mary, accusing her of laziness.

"Martha, Martha." His address is tender and affectionate, yet it has a plaintive tone. Like the time he would weep over Jerusalem, "O Jerusalem, Jerusalem . . . how often I have longed to gather your children together, as a hen gathers her chicks under her wings, but you were not willing." Or when he would prepare Peter for his fall, "Simon, Simon, Satan has asked to sift you as wheat. But I have prayed for you, Simon, that your faith may not fail." Or when he would confront Saul on the Damascus road, "Saul, Saul, why do you persecute me?"

"Martha, Martha, you are worried and upset about many things, but only one thing is needed. Mary has chosen what is better, and it will not be taken away from her."

He brings his point gently home: Fellowship with him is a matter of priorities. And a matter of choice. It's the better part of the meal life has to offer. It is, in fact, the main course.

Jesus says something extraordinary about what Mary did: it would become a permanent part of her life; it would count for eternity. Quite a promise.

And what did Mary do? All she did was sit. It is where she sat that made the difference.

Maybe it was there that she first understood what the

disciples were so slow to grasp. And maybe that's why, when they were arguing over their greatness in the kingdom, she was again at the Savior's feet—anointing him with costly perfume . . . preparing for his death with a tribute of her tears . . . saying I love you . . . and saying good-bye.

PRAYER

ear Savior at whose feet
I now sit,

When you knock on the door to my heart, what is it you are looking for? What is it you want? Is it not to come in to dine with me? Is it not for fellowship?

And yet, so often, where do you find me? At your feet? No. In the kitchen. How many times have I become distracted and left you there . . . sitting . . . waiting . . . longing?

What is so important about my kitchenful of preparations that draws me away from you? How can they seem so trivial now and yet so urgent when I'm caught up in them?

Forgive me for being so much distracted by my preparations and so little attracted by your presence. For being so diligent in my duties and so negligent in my devotion. For being so quick to my feet and so slow to yours.

Help me to understand that it is an intimate moment you seek from me, not an elaborate meal.

Guard my heart this day from the many distractions that vie for my attention. And help me to fix my eyes on you. Not on my rank in the kingdom, as did the disciples. Not on the finer points of theology, as did the scribes. Not on the sins of others, as did the Pharisees. Not on a place of worship, as did the woman at the well. Not on the budget, as did Judas. But on you.

Bring me out of the kitchen, Lord. Bid me come to your feet. And there may I thrill to sit and adore you. . . .

An
INTIMATE MOMENT
WITH
ZACCHAEUS

SCRIPTURE

Jesus entered Jericho and was passing through. A man was there by the name of Zacchaeus; he was a chief tax collector and was wealthy. He wanted to see who Jesus was, but being a short man he could not, because of the crowd. So he ran ahead and climbed a sycamore-fig tree to see him, since Jesus was coming that way.

When Jesus reached the spot, he looked up and said to him, "Zacchaeus, come down immediately. I must stay at your house today." So he came down at once and welcomed him gladly.

All the people saw this and began to mutter, "He has gone to be the guest of a 'sinner.' "

But Zacchaeus stood up and said to the Lord, "Look, Lord! Here and now I give half of my possessions to the poor, and if I have cheated anybody out of anything, I will pay back four times the amount."

Jesus said to him, "Today salvation has come to this house, because this man, too, is a son of Abraham. For the Son of Man came to seek and to save what was lost."

Luke 19:1–9

MEDITATION

Jericho. Surrounded by palms. Scented with balsam groves. Dates, palm-honey, myrrh, and balsam form a continuous caravan of exports to the East. For the Roman government, the city is a lush center of taxation. Plump. Ripe. Fragrant with revenue.

And knee-deep in the harvest are the tax collectors, making sure the proper due is rendered unto Caesar, and in the process, a denarius or two rendered unto themselves.

It is early spring in Jericho. And a chill clings to the yawning shadows that stretch across the city. For many the eastern sun is a freshly minted coin of opportunity. But commerce is far from the minds of the crowd that mingles with the morning's shadows.

For this dawn brings with it something more than the promise of commerce. It brings the promise of a Messiah.

Jesus has come to Jericho.

The crowd swells. Eddies of anticipation swirl about and gather in strength. The squeeze of the multitude grows claustrophobic as the more curious elbow for position.

But for one man, elbows aren't enough. He is Zacchaeus. A short man. So short he can't see over the crowd. So short he has to climb a tree to catch a glimpse of the procession.

Somehow this short man has survived growing up in a tall world. Growing up the object of stares. Growing up the brunt of jokes. Growing up the kid who got pushed around.

In the jostled process of growing up, a part of his

73

childhood was trodden underfoot. And that tender part of him died. Crushed under the calloused and often cruel feet of the tall. And yet he carries that stepped-on part of himself everywhere he goes. Even up the stout trunk of that sycamore tree.

But somewhere along the way to adulthood Zacchaeus learned to compensate—first, to laugh at the jokes, and later, to fight back. And so, as he climbed the professional ladder, he stepped on anyone who stood in his way, anyone on the next rung up. He would show them, show them all. Someday they'd look up to him.

At last, he made it to the top—chief tax collector. King of the hill, controlling commerce. King of the hill, greasing his greedy little palms with the sweat of the businessman's brow. King of the hill, looking down over Jericho.

But the hill he rules is a dung hill, at least in the eyes of the people. For tax gatherers are despised as ruthless bill collectors for a corrupt government. Even the Talmud looks down on them, allowing a Jew the sanction of lying to a murderer, to a thief, and . . . to a tax collector.

True, Zacchaeus has power. And he has wealth. But the stature he sought among others has eluded him. And so has friendship.

But Zacchaeus has heard stories about this Jesus who was a friend of tax collectors. Who ate and drank with them and stayed in their homes. Who changed the life of Levi, the tax collector at Capernaum. For whom Levi left a lucrative career, left everything. And not for higher wages, but for no wages at all. This Jesus must be some man. There's even talk of him being the Messiah. The thought captivates Zacchaeus: a Messiah who's a friend of tax collectors. And with a schoolboy's eagerness he shinnies up the sycamore to see him.

Zacchaeus crawls out on a limb for a better look. He marvels at the total lack of pomp and ceremony surrounding Jesus. Nothing like a king. And yet . . . and yet something about him is so regal.

People are draped over windowsills like laundry hung out to dry, watching. A thick fringe lines the rooftops and looks down. On the street are huddles of curiosity—holy men and housewives, teachers and transients, businessmen and bakers—elbow to elbow.

Suddenly Jesus stops. He looks up at Zacchaeus. Shafts of the Savior's love filter through the branches. A long-awaited dawn shines on a despised tax collector. And a strange warmth begins to stir the cold darkness of his soul.

All eyes follow Jesus as he parts the sea of spectators on his way to that sycamore. Zacchaeus feels the darkness of his soul shrinking back. For years he has rendered unto Caesar; now he must render unto Christ an account of himself.

And his soul knows that the account isn't good. The ledger is filled with entries of money extorted . . . money under the table . . . money skimmed off the top . . . money, money, money. That's the bottom line for Zacchaeus. The bottom line of a bankrupt life.

But the Savior isn't looking for an audit. He is looking

for something else. He searches Zacchaeus's eyes to find that stepped-on part of his life. And on it he sees every footprint, every heel mark. Jesus is moved with compassion for the little boy who had to grow up in a big man's world. "Zacchaeus," he calls him by name, and asks for a place to stay.

Zacchaeus locks onto the eyes that search the far reaches of his soul. They are the eyes both of a king and a friend.

Ripples of contempt work their way through the crowd. "Going where to stay? His house? Eating with a sinner?"

But the whispered innuendos can't intrude on this intimate moment.

And, in the same way you would welcome a friend you have yearned to see for a long, long time, Zacchaeus jumps down and welcomes Jesus into his home.

From behind the barriers he has erected around his heart, a flood of repentant feelings bursts forth. Feelings that had been dammed up for years. Zacchaeus goes out on still another limb. What took a lifetime to accumulate, one sentence of devotion liquidates. And not by a token ten percent. Half to the poor. Fourfold to the defrauded.

Look closely. Witness the miracle—a camel passing through the eye of a needle.

Another dawn, centuries earlier, the walls of Jericho came tumbling down at the shout of Joshua's men. Today another wall comes tumbling down in Jericho. This time, at the offer of a king's friendship. This time, the wall of a rich man's heart.

And amid the rubble, that crushed, stepped-on part of Zacchaeus's heart springs to life.

PRAYER

ear Jesus,

Forgive me for trying so long to compensate for my stunted growth. I have expected my work and my wealth to increase my stature. Help me to see, Lord, that an increase in my stature can only come as a result of a decrease in myself. It is in losing my life that I find it. It is in dying that I live. It is in giving that I receive.

I confess to you that I am short in spiritual stature. To even see you it seems that I'm always needing something to stand on.

But I want to see you. See you for who you really are. See you for myself, with my own two eyes. Not just through the eyes of a pastor. Or a teacher. Or an evangelist.

I've heard so much about you. How much is opinion? How much is hearsay? How much is truth? I want to know, for myself. I want to hear with my own ears. Not simply from a book. Or television. Or radio. Or a tape.

I'm tired of second-hand experience. I want to feel with my own heart.

If I have to climb a tree awkwardly and undignified to do so, I will gladly do it. Please come near, Lord. I'll be the one out on a limb, waiting.

And, as you come, overwhelm me with the awesome wonder that it is not I who seek you in the streets nearly as much as it is you who seeks me in the sycamores. . . .

AN
INTIMATE MOMENT
WITH
MARY

ow the Passover and the Feast of Unleavened Bread were only two days away, and the chief priests and the teachers of the law were looking for some sly way to arrest Jesus and kill him. "But not during the Feast," they said, "or the people may riot."

While he was in Bethany, reclining at the table in the home of a man known as Simon the Leper, a woman came with an alabaster jar of very expensive perfume, made of pure nard. She broke the jar and poured the perfume on his head.

Some of those present were saying indignantly to one another, "Why this waste of perfume? It could have been sold for more than a year's wages and the money given to the poor." And they rebuked her harshly.

"Leave her alone," said Jesus. "Why are you bothering her? She has done a beautiful thing to me. The poor you will always have with you, and you can help them any time you want. But you will not always have me. She did what she could. She poured perfume on my body beforehand to prepare for my burial. I tell you the truth, wherever the gospel is preached throughout the world, what she has done will also be told, in memory of her."

Then Judas Iscariot, one of the Twelve, went to the chief priests to betray Jesus to them. They were delighted to hear this and promised to give him money. So he watched for an opportunity to hand him over.

Mark 14:1–11

MEDITATION

The winds of treachery have been gusting around Jesus with increasing intensity. But there is a calm eye in the midst of this storm of mounting opposition. It is a home in Bethany, a shelter of intimate friends who come to honor him.

Parallel passages provide the guest list: Simon, a leper Jesus healed; Lazarus, a dead man Jesus raised; Martha, who served him; Mary, who sat at his feet; and, of course, the disciples, who left everything and followed him.

But a draft has made its way into this warm circle of friends, and betrayal is in the air. But only Christ feels the chill. Christ, and one other—Mary.

She comes with perfume. Expensive perfume. As she anoints him, the aroma of extravagant love fills the room. So pure. So lovely. Flowing from the veined alabaster jar of her heart, a heart broken against the hard reality of her Savior's imminent death.

Her actions are strangely out of place, a breech not only of etiquette but of a woman's place in this culture. And yet . . . are not her actions the most appropriate? Is not the breech instead being committed by the men?

Did they not see the shadow of the cross lengthening to overtake their Lord? Did they not know his hour was fast upon him?

Time and again, Jesus warned them. Both in parable— of the tenants killing the landowner's son—and in plain language:

We are going to Jerusalem, and the Son of

Man will be betrayed to the chief priests and teachers of the law. They will condemn him to death and will hand him over to the Gentiles, who will mock him and spit on him, flog him, and kill him.

How much clearer could he have spoken? What were these men thinking? Did they ignore his words? Dismiss them? Forget them? Hear only what they wanted to hear? Were the words too painful that they suppressed them? Or their minds too occupied with the work of the kingdom that they lost sight of their King?

For the disciples, the ministry was fast becoming a business to be budgeted rather than a Savior to be served.

What a stab in the heart this must have been to their honored guest. Bickering about the poor when one sits in their midst famished for a crust of human understanding. They are the most intimate confidants, yet none has a clue to the gnawing hunger inside him. Peter doesn't. James doesn't. John doesn't.

But Mary, she does. She sees the melting tallow of emotions in Christ's eyes. So beautiful the flame. So tender the wick. So mercenary the hand that seeks to extinguish it.

For this brief candle she weeps. And as she does, she anoints him with perfume to prepare for his burial.

Mingled with tears, the perfume becomes, by some mysterious chemistry of heaven, not diluted but more concentrated. Potent enough behind the ears of each century for the scent to linger to this day, a fragrant reminder of her extravagant love.

On the cross, stripped of his clothing, Jesus would wear only the perfume that Mary had lavished upon his hair. It was that perfume which filled his nostrils and covered the stench of mockers rabbled around the cross. And maybe, when he took a deep breath, it was that perfume which gave him the strength to say, "Father, forgive them, for they do not know what they are doing."

Soon the body of Jesus would be broken. Blood would spill from the whip . . . from the thorns . . . from the nails . . . and finally, from the spear thrust in his side.

A perfume more precious than nard. So pure. So lovely. So truly extravagant.

The Savior had come to earth to break an alabaster jar for humanity. And Mary had come that night to break one for him.

It was a jar he never regretted breaking.

Nor did she.

PRAYER

airest Lord Jesus,

Grant that my heart would be a Bethany for you—a quiet place of friendship where you are the honored guest.

Grant that I may respond to you not with the prudence of the disciples but with the extravagance of Mary. To realize that there is a time to sell perfume for the poor and a time to shower it on you.

Grant that where betrayal is in the air I might fill that room with a beautiful thing said or done for you. Without thought of its cost. Without thought of what others may say.

Help me, O Light of the World, to see all my possessions illumined by your presence. And to remember that their true worth is only in proportion to how they honor you. So teach me to value all you have entrusted to my care in the short life I have on this earth.

Should I ever hesitate and cling to any alabaster jar of my own, bring to my remembrance the precious jar you broke for me. And in the fragrance of that thought may I fall at your feet, as Mary did, lavishing upon you not only my treasures but also my tears. . . .

AN
INTIMATE MOMENT
WITH
JUDAS

I am not referring to all of you; I know those I have chosen. But this is to fulfill the scripture: 'He who shares my bread has lifted up his heel against me.'

"I am telling you now before it happens, so that when it does happen you will believe that I am He. I tell you the truth, whoever accepts anyone I send accepts me; and whoever accepts me accepts the one who sent me."

After he had said this, Jesus was troubled in spirit and testified, "I tell you the truth, one of you is going to betray me."

His disciples stared at one another, at a loss to know which of them he meant. One of them, the disciple whom Jesus loved, was reclining next to him. Simon Peter motioned to this disciple and said, "Ask him which one he means."

Leaning back against Jesus, he asked him, "Lord, who is it?"

Jesus answered, "It is the one to whom I will give this piece of bread when I have dipped it in the dish." Then, dipping the piece of bread, he gave it to Judas Iscariot, son of Simon. As soon as Judas took the bread, Satan entered into him.

"What you are about to do, do quickly," Jesus told him, but no one at the meal understood why Jesus said this to him. Since Judas had charge of the money, some thought Jesus was telling him to buy what was needed for the Feast, or to give something to the poor. As soon as Judas had taken the bread, he went out. And it was night.

John 13:18–30

MEDITATION

Judas Iscariot. Just saying the name leaves a bitter aftertaste on the tongue. For it is a name synonymous with the most treacherous of betrayals—the betrayal of a friend.

He was chosen as one of the Twelve to follow Jesus for three and a half years. But in spite of all he heard, in spite of all he saw, even in spite of Jesus Himself, Judas followed only as far as the gate of the kingdom. No farther. He never could quite take that step of faith to enter in.

What a tragedy. Feet that walked so close to Christ, yet a heart that lagged behind at such a distance.

Hard to imagine, isn't it? But, then again, it all makes perfect sense, knowing Judas.

For Judas was a practical man.

He was the disciple with the best business head on his shoulders—budget-minded, pragmatic, utilitarian. That's why he held the purse strings to the ministry. And that is why, when Mary anointed Jesus with costly perfume, he rebuked the extravagance. Ostensibly on behalf of the poor. But, in reality, on behalf of himself. For he held the purse with a pilfering hand, and he saw the extravagance as money out of his pocket.

When the tide of popularity had turned against Jesus, Judas had started looking ahead, taking precautions to protect himself. Socking away a little more money here and there. Just in case.

For Judas was a practical man.

To make things worse, Jesus started pointing a finger at the religious hierarchy, people with influence, people with power. And that just wasn't done in Jerusalem. By anybody.

Within that inner circle seethed a caldron of hate for the brash young preacher. Stirred by a twisted combination of jealousy and paranoia, a plot brewed and soon thickened. Jesus would have to be killed. Once Judas got wind of the plot, his calculating mind went straight to the bottom line: *If they kill Jesus, certainly we Twelve will be next on their list.*

He didn't look at his shift of loyalties as betrayal. If Jesus was determined to dig his own grave, Judas thought, he was just helping him with the shovel, that's all. Merely a practical matter of hurrying along the inevitable and looking out for himself. Was there dishonor in jumping from a sinking ship? And the thirty pieces of silver? Well, that was just a life preserver, a little something to keep him afloat until he could find a place to dry off somewhere. Preferably a warm, comfortable place in the religious hierarchy. Treasurer maybe?

Such thoughts Judas secrets away in his heart as they enter Jerusalem. He has been able to hide his true identity from the other disciples. Until tonight. Tonight the mask would come off.

As the disciples prepare for Passover, Jerusalem is brimming with religious pilgrims who have poured into the holy city to celebrate the feast. It is a sacred time for the Jew. A time to look back—back to the nation's deliverance from the tight-knuckled, four-hundred-year grip of Egyptian bondage. It is also a time to look forward—forward to the time when the Messiah will come to usher in an unprecedented era of blessing.

This Passover, Jesus and the Twelve withdraw to an upper room. It is a quiet respite from tonight's teeming crowds—and from the turbulent storm that awaits tomorrow.

In his soul Jesus feels the sharp winds which harbinger that storm. He feels the chill of betrayal, of desertion, of denial.

Jesus and the disciples gather around a low table to celebrate the feast. John reclines to the right of Jesus; Judas, to the left at the place of honor. They stretch slantwise on padded mats, propping themselves on the left arm, leaving the other free to handle the food.

Each portion they handle is a sermoned echo of the nation's first Passover. The bowl of bitter herbs, vinegar, and salt is a reminder of the bitter years of slavery. The flat cakes of yeastless bread are a reminder of their hurried exodus. And finally, there is the roasted lamb, a symbol of deliverance.

What broke Pharaoh's oppressive fist that first Passover was a final, climactic plague—a visit from the angel of death to kill every firstborn son. To spare the Jews from that fate, God instructed them to kill a lamb and sprinkle its blood on the sides and tops of the doorframes outside their homes. When the angel of death saw this evidence of faith, it passed over that house and traveled on to another.

Tonight, Jesus is celebrating the feast an evening early. For tomorrow, when the nation will be preparing its Passover lambs, God will be preparing his. An innocent lamb, without spot or blemish . . . led to the slaughter, silent before its shearers . . . stricken, pierced for our transgressions.

His blood will be sprinkled on wooden crossbeams outside the city. And all Jerusalem will behold the Lamb of God that takes away the sin of the world.

Several oil lamps dot that upper room, sending a gallery of shadows to watch from the walls. Satan is among them, watching, gloating, waiting for the opportune moment to step from behind those shadows.

Earlier in that room Jesus had washed the disciples' feet, teaching them a final lesson about serving. Two of those feet belonged to Judas. So calloused the heels. Yet so tender the hands that washed them. How convicting it must have been for Judas. And how crushing for Jesus.

Seated now at the table, Jesus' forehead is furrowed, his brows knit, his eyes intense. He has so much to tell his disciples. But so little time. A hush falls over the room as he speaks, "He who shares my bread has lifted up his heel against me."

It has been said that forgiveness is the fragrance the violet sheds on the heel that crushed it. Could there be a fragrance as sweet in all the world as that of Jesus having washed the very heel that was poised to crush him?

A tremor of remorse unsettles the Savior's spirit. It is his task to unmask the traitor. A task he takes no delight in.

"I tell you the truth, one of you is going to betray me."

At the mention of a traitor in their midst, the disciples recoil, shadows miming every move. At first, there is only a tense, breathless silence. Then the table is abuzz with whispered questions regarding the traitor's identity.

"It is the one to whom I will give this piece of bread when I have dipped it in the dish."

It was customary for the master of the feast to put bits of lamb onto a piece of unleavened bread, dip it into the bitter herb sauce, and hand it to his guests. And it was customary to offer the first piece to the most honored guest.

He hands the bread to Judas . . . to take . . . and to eat.

The dramatic moment is not only an unmasking of the traitor but a final offer of salvation. Judas's pulse quickens and his face flushes hot and red. For an awkward moment, the eyes of the betrayer and the betrayed meet. A knife of regret cuts an opening in Judas's soul. Haltingly, he takes the rolled-up piece of bread. But he can't quite bring it to his mouth. Sweat gathers at his hairline. He bites his lip.

From the shadows Satan sees the quivering hand. He sees his pawn is vulnerable. The Prince of Darkness counters with a stategic move and enters Judas.

The disciple puts down the bread and reaches for his pouch. The opening is closed. The pawn is safe.

"What you are about to do, do quickly."

With those words, Jesus seals his fate. And the fate of

Judas. They would both go their separate ways. To separate trees. To separate destinies.

"What you are about to do, do quickly."

It would be the last command Judas would obey. And it would be the last intimate moment he would spend with the Savior.

Ever.

For Judas was a practical man.

PRAYER

ear Man of Sorrows,

How painful that last supper must have been for you. How your heart must have broken.

Thank you for offering yourself, O Lamb of God, as a sacrifice for sin. Thank you for sprinkling your blood on the beams of that cross so my iniquities might be passed over. And thank you for the exodus you brought about in my life, an exodus from the harsh Egypt where I was once a slave.

Lord, when I read of Judas, I can't help but see something of myself in him. Something that keeps my hands clutched to my purse strings. Something obsessively practical that keeps me from letting go and following you completely.

Thank you that you see the traitor in me, too, and yet still you love . . . still you wash the foot whose heel is set against you . . . still you offer bread to lips whose kiss would betray you.

I am unworthy of so great a love, dear Lord Jesus.

Grant that love so pure would change my life. That it would loosen my grip on material things. That it would free me from serving two masters. That it would help me to serve—and love—only you.

O Lord, help me to love my enemies and to pray for those who persecute me or who, in some way, betray me. Help me not to trade insult for insult or injury for injury. Help me to give a blessing instead. Help me to be a friend who loves as you did at that Last Supper—a friend who loves to the end, even when that love is refused. . . .

ANOTHER
INTIMATE MOMENT
WITH
PETER

SCRIPTURE

imon, Simon, Satan has asked to sift you as wheat. But I have prayed for you, Simon, that your faith may not fail. And when you have turned back, strengthen your brothers."

But he replied, "Lord, I am ready to go with you to prison and to death."

Jesus answered, "I tell you, Peter, before the rooster crows today, you will deny three times that you know me. . . ."

Then seizing [Jesus], they led him away and took him into the house of the high priest. Peter followed at a distance. But when they had kindled a fire in the middle of the courtyard and had sat down together, Peter sat down with them. A servant girl saw him seated there in the firelight. She looked closely at him and said, "This man was with him."

But he denied it. "Woman, I don't know him," he said.

A little later someone else saw him and said, "You also are one of them."

"Man, I am not!" Peter replied. About an hour later another asserted, "Certainly this fellow was with him, for he is a Galilean."

Peter replied, "Man, I don't know what you're talking about!" Just as he was speaking, the rooster crowed. The Lord turned and looked straight at Peter. Then Peter remembered the word the Lord had spoken to him: "Before the rooster crows today, you will disown me three times." And he went outside and wept bitterly.

Luke 22:31–34, 54–62

MEDITATION

In the course of the evening, the disciples would go from arguing over their greatness in the kingdom to deserting their king. Jesus warned them it would happen: "This very night you will all fall away on account of me, for it is written:

"'I will strike the shepherd, and the sheep of the flock will be scattered.' "

It happened just as he said. The pack of blood-thirsty wolves came, their teeth bared for the kill. They led away the Good Shepherd, who, with crimson love, would lay down his life for the sheep. The sheep, meanwhile, huddled themselves away in cold, frightened bunches of twos and threes.

Only two of the disciples dared to backtrack and trail Jesus as he was being led away. One was John, the disciple Jesus loved; the other, Peter.

Peter—the Gibralter among the disciples. Tonight that rock would crumble. Tonight he would be reduced to a mere pebble of a man.

He would start the evening in a resolute posture in the upper room, "Lord, I am ready to go with you to prison and to death. Even if all fall away on account of you, I will never fall away." Later in the night he would stand single-handedly against a mob of Roman soldiers, wielding his sword in the torch-lit garden of Gethsemane. But before dawn, he wouldn't even be able to stand up to the stares of a young servant girl.

What could account for so great a defection from so

97

dedicated a disciple?

The answer is carefully wrapped in words both plaintive and tender, "Simon, Simon, Satan has asked to sift
you as wheat." The implied conversation between Jesus
and Satan is reminiscent of the permission Satan obtained
from God to test Job.

> "Does Job fear God for nothing?" Satan
> replied. "Have you not put a hedge around
> him and his household and everything he has?
> You have blessed the work of his hands, so
> that his flocks and herds are spread through-
> out the land. But stretch out your hand and
> strike everything he has, and he will surely
> curse you to your face."
> The Lord said to Satan, "Very well, then,
> everything he has is in your hands, but on
> the man himself do not lay a finger."

Tonight, into those hands Peter would fall. Satan wants
to thresh his faith and beat it into the ground until the
husk breaks open. Then he'll show the world what's really
inside Peter's heart. And once the other disciples see this,
the backbone of the revolution will be as good as crushed.

The hour is late; the night, dark and chilly. Peter has
followed Jesus all the way to the temple courtyard where
the Savior, under heavy guard, awaits his hearing. He
comes because Jesus is his Lord, because Jesus would have
come for him had the tables been turned. He comes to
help, not knowing what he can do, or how, or when. A
thousand scenarios crowd his mind. He is confused and

torn. *Do I grab a sword and fight? No, he rebuked me for that in the garden. Do I testify on his behalf? A lot of good that would do. Do I just watch and listen so I can rally the disciples in the morning?*

Cloaked in anonymity, Peter comes to warm himself by a campfire, a radius of warmth shared by his Lord's captors. He comes to think, to sort things out, to plan his next move.

He sits, pushing his palms against the heat, rubbing his arms. He takes from the fire its warmth and the idle companionship of strangers small-talking the evening away.

Talk around the fire crackles with news of the Nazarene's arrest. They point to Jesus as they talk and nod and lay odds on his chances. Snakes of fire slither upward and hiss, licking the night air. By the light of these flames, Satan will do his work. A servant girl squints at Peter through the uncertain light cast by the fire.

"This man was with him."

Peter feels the heat of the incriminating flames and flatly denies the charge. He begins to sweat now. *What good would I be to Jesus if my identity was out in the open? It would only make matters worse. And who would get word back to the others?*

Sometime later there is another accusation. And immediately another denial, only more forceful this time. Finally, his accent gives him away.

"You're a Galilean, I can tell by the way you talk. You must be one of his disciples."

He would have to think quick to get around that one. He then curses and swears, letting loose a herd of expletives in hopes of kicking up enough dust to cloud his identity. In no uncertain terms he denies any association with Jesus. The ploy seems to have worked. The circle around the campfire appears satisfied.

But somewhere in the night a rooster stretches its neck, shakes its feathers, and crows an indictment.

The disciple jerks his head around and catches Jesus looking at him. It is a brief moment, almost too short to be intimate. But a moment like this has a way of stretching and framing itself to hang in the mind.

The Savior utters no words. Nor does he shake his head in disgust. Or lower it in disappointment. His look is not a begrudged I-told-you-so. It is sympathetic, from one who knows what it's like to fall into the winnowing hands of Satan. Jesus has been there, too. For forty days in a barren wilderness. He knows how hard the winnow is and how ruthless the adversary's hand that holds it. No, his look carries no grudge. It is the look of a friend who understands.

With that look, all of Peter's pent-up emotions suddenly cave in on themselves. He runs from the courtyard, bitter tears stinging his eyes. He stops somewhere outside and beats his fists against his chest. He pulls at his hair. He gnarls his face. The weight of his guilt is too much to bear. He collapses in a wailing heap.

He weeps for the Savior he has so miserably failed.

And he weeps for himself. *O God, no, no, no. What have I done? What have I done? God, take this one dark hour from me. Turn back the night. Give me another chance. Please, O God. Turn back the night.*

But the night will not be turned back. And this darkest of hours will not be taken from him.

When the tears finally do stop, the night has paled to gray. Soon it will be dawn.

The winnowing is over. All that is left is the naked kernel of faith. It is a small grain, but a grain Satan couldn't touch. He could winnow all the chaff he wanted, but the wheat belongs to Jesus.

Peter is a smaller man now without the thick husk that once surrounded his life. He is broken and he is bare.

Be hard on him if you like. Talk about how self-confident he was. Talk about how impulsive he was. Talk about how he was always shooting off his mouth. And how he needed a good sifting.

Go ahead.

But before you do, remember that the other disciples had already deserted Jesus. Peter and John alone followed him that terrifying night.

True, Peter followed him at a distance. But still he followed. Yes, he was rash in drawing his sword in the garden. He did it mistakenly. But he did it against insurmountable odds, at almost certain loss of his own life.

And it's true, he failed Jesus. But he failed in a court-yard where the others dared not set foot. And he failed not under normal pressure, but under the heavy winnow of Satan.

So go ahead. Be hard on him. But remember, it was Satan, not Jesus, who did the sifting.

Jesus was the friend who prayed.

PRAYER

ear Lord Jesus,

Thank you for Peter. He was a great man. He loved you so much. He left everything to follow you. In your name he healed the sick, cast out demons, and preached the kingdom. For three and a half faithful years he stood beside you. And when the soldiers came to take you away, he stood up for you. When the others deserted you, he followed all the way to the temple courtyard.

I confess I would have never made it that far.

Help me not to pass judgment on him, Lord. Rather, may his great and fervent love for you pass judgment on me.

Help me to see that I deny you in so many areas of my life, in so many ways and at so many different times.

> When I am too busy to pray, I deny that you are the center of my life.
> When I neglect your Word, I deny that you are competent to guide me.
> When I worry, I deny that you are Lord of my circumstances.
> When I turn my head from the hungry and the homeless, I deny that you are a God of mercy who has put me here to be your hands and your feet.
> When I steal something from another person to enrich or enhance my life—whether that be something material or some credit that is rightly due another, which I have claimed for myself—I deny you are the source of all blessings.

Forgive me, Jesus, for all those quiet ways, known only to you, in which I have denied you.

Help me to pray for and encourage others the way you did for Peter. Even during those times when they may in some way deny their friendship. Especially during those times.

Thank you for all the times you have prayed for me that my faith might not fail. There is no telling how many times I have been rescued from Satan's hand because you stood beside me. And thank you, most faithful of friends, that no matter how terribly I have failed you, I can always look into your eyes, and there find forgiveness. . . .

AN
INTIMATE MOMENT
WITH A
THIEF ON THE CROSS

Two other men, both criminals, were also led out with him to be executed. When they came to the place called the Skull, there they crucified him, along with the criminals—one on his right, the other on his left. Jesus said, "Father, forgive them, for they do not know what they are doing." And they divided up his clothes by casting lots.

The people stood watching, and the rulers even sneered at him. They said, "He saved others; let him save himself if he is the Christ of God, the Chosen One."

The soldiers also came up and mocked him. They offered him wine vinegar and said, "If you are the king of the Jews, save yourself."

There was a written notice above him, which read: THIS IS THE KING OF THE JEWS.

One of the criminals who hung there hurled insults at him: "Aren't you the Christ? Save yourself and us!"

But the other criminal rebuked him. "Don't you fear God," he said, "since you are under the same sentence? We are punished justly, for we are getting what our deeds deserve. But this man has done nothing wrong."

Then he said, "Jesus, remember me when you come into your kingdom."

Jesus answered him, "I tell you the truth, today you will be with me in paradise."

Luke 23:32–43

MEDITATION

The cross stands like a set of scales silhouetted against the Jerusalem sky. Its upraised stanchion balances a crossbeam where love and justice meet, where all humanity has been weighed—and found wanting.

There Jesus hangs with outstretched arms, aching for a prodigal world's return.

On either side hang two thieves, teetering between life and death, between heaven and hell. Teetering until one, at last, reaches out in faith, "Remember me when you come into your kingdom."

It is the last kind word said to Jesus before he dies, spoken not by a religious leader, nor by the disciple whom he loved, nor even by his mother standing at his feet, but by a common thief.

And with the words, "Today you will be with me in paradise," that thief is lifted off those weighted scales and into the waiting arms of the Savior.

We know nothing about that criminal on the cross next to Christ. We don't know how much he stole or how often. From whom or why. We know only that he was a thief—a wayward son over whom some mother's heart has been broken; over whom some father's hopes have been dashed.

But we know one other thing.

From Matthew's account, we know that he joined with the crowd in mocking Jesus:

"He saved others, but he can't save himself!
He's the King of Israel! Let him come down

now from the cross, and we will believe in him. He trusts in God. Let God rescue him now if he wants him, for he said, 'I am the Son of God.'" In the same way the robbers who were crucified with him also heaped insults on him.

"In the same way the robbers"—plural. They both joined in the sneering and taunting.

Question: What happens to change that one thief's heart—to give him the heroism to stand up for Jesus and the humility to submit to him?

Answer: He hears at arm's distance what Peter hears from afar and would write about years later:

When they hurled their insults at him, he did not retaliate; when he suffered, he made no threats. Instead, he entrusted himself to him who judges justly.

In the midst of the spears of abuse thrust into Jesus' side, this thief hears him appeal to a court higher than Caesar's. The appeal is not for justice but for mercy. And not mercy for himself but for his accusers. The spears are sharp and relentless, but Jesus does not throw them back. He bears them in his heart.

The one outlaw hears all this and lifts his faint head to look at the man from whose lips these tender words came. And when his eyes meet the Savior's, for a moment all time stands still. In those eyes he sees no hatred, no scorn, no judgment. He sees only one thing—forgiveness.

Then he knows. He is face to face with a dying God.

That thief didn't know much theology. He only knew three things: that Jesus was a king, that his kingdom was not of this world, and that this king had the power to bring even the most unworthy into his kingdom.

But that was enough.

And, in an intimate moment with the Savior, a lifetime of moral debt is cancelled.

Incredible, when you think of it. Amidst the humiliating abuse of the crowd and the excruciating pain of the cross, Jesus was still about his Father's business. Even with his eyes sinking on the feverish horizon of death, he was telling a common thief about the uncommon riches of heaven.

PRAYER

ear Jesus,

Help me to look at you through the eyes of that thief on the cross. And grant me the grace, I pray, to see in your eyes the forgiveness that he saw.

For I, too, have stolen much. When I have gossiped, I have taken from another's reputation, and in the process, robbed from my own. When I have raised my voice in anger, I have taken something away from peace. When I have aided and abetted immoral thoughts, I have stolen from another's dignity, depreciating that person from a sacred object of your love to a common object of my own lust. When I have hurt someone's feelings, I have taken something from that person's self-worth—something which might never be replaced, something for which I might never be able to make restitution. When I have spoken the truth, but not in love, I have stolen from your kingdom by pushing a soul, not closer, but farther away from the borders of paradise.

Remember me, O King, a common thief.

I stand before you naked in the shame of a squandered life—and I ask you to clothe me. I stand before you with a gnawing hunger in my soul—and I ask you to feed me. I stand before you thirsting for forgiveness—and I ask you to touch but a drop of your tender mercies to my parched lips.

Grant me the grace to live such a life that when you do remember me in your kingdom, O Lord, you may remember me with a smile, and look forward to the day when I, too, will be with you in paradise. . . .

An
Intimate Moment
With The
Savior's Mother

SCRIPTURE

Near the cross of Jesus stood his mother, his mother's sister, Mary the wife of Clopas, and Mary Magdalene. When Jesus saw his mother there, and the disciple whom he loved standing nearby, he said to his mother, "Dear woman, here is your son," and to the disciple, "Here is your mother." From that time on, this disciple took her into his home.

John 19:25–27

MEDITATION

As Mary stares at the cross, it blurs in a teary mist and seems like the hilt of a sword plunged into the heart of the earth. As she ponders the image, the cryptic words of Simeon, spoken at Jesus' birth, come rushing back to her:

> "This child is destined to cause the falling and rising of many in Israel, and to be a sign that will be spoken against, so that the thoughts of many will be revealed. And a sword shall pierce your own soul too."

As the cross comes into focus again, it dawns on her: So *this* is the sword.

It is something every mother fears—losing a child. That fear has haunted her ever since Simeon's foreboding words. Then there was the terror of Herod's assassination plot on the baby. And the Suffering Servant prophecy in Isaiah has always troubled her. It was as if Death had perched on Jesus' crib since his birth, casting its dark shadow as a reminder that one day the boy would be his.

Deep down inside, Mary knew that Jesus was a child born to die. He would not grow up to be a doctor or a lawyer or a rabbi. He would not marry or give her grandchildren to carry on the family name. She's known this for a long time now and has buried it in her heart.

In pools of tears swim a few tender memories. His birth in that cold, dark stable in Bethlehem. How he shivered as she held him for the first time, so tiny and helpless. How her breast warmed him. How her song lulled him to sleep. And how, when she kissed his forehead, he looked so peaceful, without a care in the world.

The cross comes into focus again, and she sees crude, hunched-over men gambling their souls away as they cast lots for his clothes. She looks up at her son and aches. He is naked, and there is no one to warm him. He is thirsty, and there is no one to wet his lips. He is tired, and there is no one to sing him to sleep. His forehead is wrinkled in agony, and there is no one to kiss it, no one to mop his care-ridden brow.

What did my baby ever do to deserve this?

Again her eyes blur. Another memory floats by. And another. She remembers his first word. She remembers his first step. She remembers how he used to love to help her bake, and how she would pull off a portion of fresh bread, dip it in honey, and give it to him. She remembers how it made her little boy smile and his eyes sparkle.

What did my little boy ever do to deserve this?

She remembers when he was twelve and already about his Father's business at the temple in Jerusalem. She distinctly remembers thinking then, *He's not my little boy anymore.*

A mother's love, that's why she is there.

A Savior's love, that's why he is.

But love never looked like this. Pools of blood beading the dirt beneath the cross. A heavy spike through the feet. Ribs protruding against the skin. Open wounds bothered by flies. Eyes swollen with fever. Hair matted from this morning's thorns. Hands raised to God on splintered wood. A slumped torso, dangling from impaled wrists like some grotesque pendant.

This is what his mother sees as she bares her heart to the hilt of that cruel, Roman sword. It is more than a mother can bear. But somehow she does. Largely because of the man standing beside her, steadying her—John, the disciple Jesus loves. Arm in arm, the two people Jesus loves the most in the whole world. They were never closer to each other than they are now, at this very moment.

They hear Jesus groan as he raises his head. He shapes his farewell with a tongue that is parched and lips that are split. John leads Mary closer to spare Jesus the strain, for her son has so much to tell to her: *Thank you for everything . . . I owe you so much . . . you've been as dear a mother as anyone could ask for.*

But the spasms in his chest are more frequent, and those feelings go unspoken. Jesus pushes on the spike and struggles to fill his lungs. The pain is excruciating. His words come at great effort.

"Dear woman, here is your son."

She looks to John and clutches his arm as fresh wells of tears pool in her eyes. Her lips squeeze out a trembled smile.

"John, here is your mother."

The disciple nods as he bites his lip to fight back the emotion. That is all that is said. For an intimate moment they behold the one they love so much. Then Jesus slumps again, his heavy eyes closing.

Suddenly, Mary realizes, *He is about his Father's business.*

She prays to that Father, prays that death would come quickly to her son. No, *their* son. For both would lose a child today. Both would bear the blade in their breast.

Yet in spite of her grief, in spite of the cold steel sheathed in her heart, she is standing near that cross. She can't bear to watch. But she can't bear to turn away either. She is there. Standing by her son. As any mother would.

She was there when he came into this world. She would be there when he left it. She was there when he was pushed through a dark and constricting birth canal and into her arms. She would be there now as he is being pushed through another painful passage, returning him to the arms of his Father.

PRAYER

ear Man of Sorrows,

Who, with the weight of your body pulling against those nails and the weight of the world's sin pulling against your soul, thought more of the sorrows of others than your own.

Who was such a compelling commentary on the only commandment with a promise, all the while knowing that for you that promise would be withheld.

Who was stripped of everything, yet still found so much to give: to your executioners, forgiveness; to a thief, paradise; to your mother, a son.

Grant me the grace, O Lord, that I would never forget how you rose above your forsakenness to make sure your mother would not be forsaken. What an example of selfless love. What an example of everything a son should be.

Keep me from ever wandering far from the foot of that cross. For that is the fountain where love is most pure. That is where I am cleansed, not only from my sin but from my pettiness. That is where I am closest to you. That is where I am closest to those who love you. Bring me there daily, Lord. That is where love is. And that is where I need to be. . . .

An
INTIMATE MOMENT
WITH
JOSEPH AND NICODEMUS

SCRIPTURE

Later, Joseph of Arimathea asked Pilate for the body of Jesus. Now Joseph was a disciple of Jesus, but secretly because he feared the Jews. With Pilate's permission, he came and took the body away. He was accompanied by Nicodemus, the man who earlier had visited Jesus at night. Nicodemus brought a mixture of myrrh and aloes, about seventy-five pounds. Taking Jesus' body, the two of them wrapped it, with the spices, in strips of linen. This was in accordance with Jewish burial customs. At the place where Jesus was crucified, there was a garden, and in the garden a new tomb, in which no one had ever been laid. Because it was the Jewish day of Preparation and since the tomb was nearby, they laid Jesus there.

John 19:38–42

MEDITATION

arkness entombs Jerusalem. A great light has gone out of the world.

Jesus is dead.

Normally, the dead are left on the cross as food for the vultures and wild dogs, as a tacit reminder that crimes against the Empire don't pay.

But the religious leaders have asked that the bodies be removed before sundown. Before their holy day begins. Especially since this Sabbath is the holiest of days for them—Passover. Such irony. So calloused in their killing of the Savior, yet so careful in their keeping of the Sabbath.

Ironic also that it is religious leaders who come to bury Jesus—two who didn't consent to the plan.

The men are among Israel's most influential. Joseph of Arimathea—a rich and prominent member of the Jewish ruling council. And Nicodemus—also a member of the council, a Pharisee, and the preeminent teacher in Israel.

They are good and upright men, waiting for the kingdom of God. They are seekers of truth, which is why they had sought out Jesus. Nicodemus had come to him at night with his questions. Joseph had become a disciple, only a secret one for fear of the Jews.

Both have kept their relationship with him in the shadows. They feared the controversy and the consequences of making their faith public. But now that Jesus is dead, a new boldness emerges in their lives. Joseph goes directly to Pilate for permission to give Jesus a proper burial. To Pilate, the very man who sent him to the cross.

Permission granted, Joseph comes with the linen; Nicodemus, with the spices. They hurry, as Jesus must be buried before sundown trumpets in the Sabbath.

Coming to the cross, they are stunned to view the lifeless slump of torn flesh that was once such a vital Savior. A sudden wave of emotion crashes against them, and they fall to their knees. They weep for Jesus. They weep for the world that did this. And they weep for themselves. For all they didn't say. For all they didn't do. For all the times they stayed in the shadows.

Joseph plants a ladder under the crossbeam and ascends with uncertain steps. Timidly at first, for this is not the work of a rich man, he wrestles with the stubborn nail in Jesus' wrist.

Nicodemus watches from the ground. His robe is swept by a sudden gust of wind, and the words Jesus spoke to him that one windswept night rustle in his mind: "Just as Moses lifted up the snake in the desert, so the Son of Man must be lifted up."

Lifted up. The words thumb through his encyclopedic mind and come to a stop in Isaiah, the prophecy of the Suffering Servant.

My servant will be . . . lifted up.

Awkwardly, Joseph lowers the body to the outstretched arms of Nicodemus, who steadies himself under the weight. His arms tremble as they wrap around Jesus' lacerated back, slick with blood.

They put the body on the ground and stand back to

get a hold of themselves. They survey the damage the Romans have done. The body lies there, pathetically, in a twisted pose. His head is punctured from Jerusalem thorns. His face, swollen and discolored from Roman fists. His shoulders, pulled out of socket from the gravity of the last six hours. His hands and feet—bored and rasped by seven-inch spikes—expose ragged muscles and white bone. His back and rib cage, clawed from a savage cat-o'-nine-tails.

Nicodemus sees before him the incarnation of Isaiah's words:

> *his appearance was so disfigured*
> *beyond that of any man*
> *and his form marred*
> *beyond human likeness—*

Nicodemus looks at the blood on his own hands and robe and pensively quotes from that prophecy:

"so will he sprinkle many nations."

The two kneel beside this servant who has suffered so much, and they gingerly work their wet cloths over his blood-stained body. Nicodemus continues:

"He was despised and rejected by men,
    a man of sorrows, and familiar with
    suffering.
Like one from whom men hide their faces
    he was despised, and we esteemed him not."

In the quiet courtroom of their hearts, they realize that loving Jesus in private was just another way of despising him and esteeming him not. And their hearts condemn them for their sins of omission.

Sponging down the rib cage, Joseph's hand touches the gouge made by the spear. He looks solemnly at Nicodemus as he, too, recalls Isaiah's words:

"He was pierced for our transgressions."

The descending sun hurries their work. They wrap the body with strips of linen, layered with aromatic spices. Both are ashamed for not doing more to prevent this brutal tragedy. They had influence. Their words carried weight. They could have objected more forcefully. They could have warned the disciples. They could have done something. Anything. But no, they had their careers to worry about.

Shouldering this guilt, they pick up the body to take it to Joseph's tomb. Suddenly, Nicodemus remembers one other thing from Isaiah's words:

"He was assigned a grave with the wicked,
and with the rich in his death."

It's as if Jesus graciously gave them the verse. For as Nicodemus says this, he looks at Joseph, and they realize that they *have* done something. They have spared the Savior the shame of a criminal's burial, where he would have been thrown into the garbage dump outside the city.

For these most unlikely of heroes, this is their most passionate hour. An hour when hatred against Jesus is most intense. An hour when friendship with him is most dangerous. This is the hour of late blooming love that draws them out of the shadows . . . to fearlessly befriend their Savior.

PRAYER

ear Suffering Servant,

How they have marred and disfigured you. How they have despised and rejected you. How you have suffered.

As I see you there on that cross, I fall to my knees, knowing that where I stand is sacred ground. Thank you for being pierced for our transgressions and crushed for our iniquities. Thank you that in your blood there is cleansing and in your wounds there is healing.

I pray that standing at the foot of your cross would do for me what it did for Joseph and Nicodemus—that your love would completely overwhelm me and draw me to you. Regardless of what others may say. Regardless of what consequences I may have to suffer. For whatever the consequences, they pale by comparison to what you suffered for me.

For me.

I can hardly comprehend such a love. Love that came so costly to you and yet so freely to me.

To me, one so fearful. To me, one so long in the shadows.

Thank you for the power of the cross, a power that can draw cowards out of the shadows and turn them into heroes.

Help me to realize that a late blooming love is better than a love that doesn't bloom at all. And help me to realize that even a late blooming love—whether that of a thief on the cross or that of a religious leader on the ruling council—even a late blooming love is fragrant and beautiful to you. . . .

An
INTIMATE MOMENT
WITH
MARY MAGDALENE

SCRIPTURE

Early on the first day of the week, while it was still dark, Mary Magdalene went to the tomb and saw that the stone had been removed from the entrance. So she came running to Simon Peter and the other disciple, the one Jesus loved, and said, "They have taken the Lord out of the tomb, and we don't know where they have put him!"

So Peter and the other disciple started for the tomb. Both were running, but the other disciple outran Peter and reached the tomb first. He bent over and looked in at the strips of linen lying there but did not go in. Then Simon Peter, who was behind him, arrived and went into the tomb. He saw the strips of linen lying there, as well as the burial cloth that had been around Jesus' head. The cloth was folded up by itself, separate from the linen. Finally the other disciple, who had reached the tomb first, also went inside. He saw and believed. (They still did not understand from Scripture that Jesus had to rise from the dead.)

Then the disciples went back to their homes, but Mary stood outside the tomb crying. As she wept, she bent over to look into the tomb and saw two angels in white, seated where Jesus' body had been, one at the head and the other at the foot.

They asked her, "Woman, why are you crying?"

"They have taken my Lord away," she said, "and I don't know where they have put him." At this, she turned around and saw Jesus standing there, but she did not realize that it was Jesus.

"Woman," he said, "why are you crying? Who is it you are looking for?"

Thinking he was the gardener, she said, "Sir, if you have carried him away, tell me where you have put him, and I will get him."

Jesus said to her, "Mary."

She turned toward him and cried out in Aramaic, "Rabboni!" (which means Teacher).

Jesus said, "Do not hold on to me, for I have not yet returned to the Father. Go instead to my brothers and tell them, 'I am returning to my Father and your Father, to my God and your God.' "

Mary Magdalene went to the disciples with the news: "I have seen the Lord!" And she told them that he had said these things to her.

John 20:1–18

MEDITATION

It was in a garden ages ago that paradise was lost, and it is in a garden now that it would be regained.

But Mary Magdalene doesn't know that. For her, the hobnail boot of the Roman Empire has crushed her hope and ground it in the dirt with its iron heel.

Her hope was Jesus. He had changed her life, and she had followed him ever since. He had cast seven demons out of her, freeing her from untold torment. He had given her life . . . a reason to live . . . a place in his kingdom. He had given her worth and dignity . . . understanding . . . compassion . . . love . . . and he had given her hope.

Now that hope lies at the bottom of her heart, flat and lifeless.

But something helps her survive the cruel boot. Something resilient, like a blade of grass that springs up after being stepped on.

That something is love.

Love brought Mary to his cross. And love brings her now to his grave.

But as she wends her way along that dark garden path, she stumbles upon a chilling sight. The stone has been rolled away. The tomb has been violated.

Just when she thinks life couldn't get worse, it gets worse. The night gets darker; her hope grows dimmer.

As she runs to tell the disciples, a legion of questions haunts her. *Who took the body? The Roman government?*

The religious leaders? But why? What would they want with it? Have they given him to the dogs by throwing him outside the city in the garbage dumps of the Valley of Gehenna? Have they put him on display to further mock him?

She finds Peter and John and in breathless fragments reports what she saw. They rip through the night on a ragged footrace to the tomb. Mary tries to follow, but her side is splitting. She will catch up, she tells herself, when she catches her breath.

His lungs burning, Peter stoops into the caved entrance. The wings of the dove-gray dawn have extended a soft feather of light into the cave. As his eyes adjust, he takes careful notice of the burial wrappings made rigid by the resin from the spices. The linen cocoon lays intact on the stone slab. Intact, but hollow.

Doubt and faith swirl in their minds like heady wine, blurring their perception as they stumble their way through the dark. Mary is left behind; tears, her only companions. She takes those tears with her as she enters the tomb to take a look for herself. And suddenly, the woman who was once possessed with demons finds herself in the presence of angels.

One stands at the head of the stone slab; the other, at the foot. Like the ark of the covenant in the Most Holy Place of the tabernacle—cherubim on either end. For this, too, is a most holy place.

She is despondent as she tells them the reason for her tears. Then, from behind, another voice reaches out to her,

"Woman, why are you crying?"

131

She wheels around. Maybe the morning is foggy. Maybe tears blur her eyes. Maybe Jesus is the last person she expects to see. Whatever the reason, she doesn't recognize him. That is, until—

"Mary."

She blinks away the tears and can hardly believe her eyes.

"Master."

Overwhelmed, she throws her arms around the Lord she loves so much. She had been there when he suffered at the cross; now he is there when she is suffering. She had stood by him in his darkest hour; now he is standing by her in hers. He had seen her tears; now he is there to wipe them all away. Jesus interrupts the embrace to send her to the disciples with the good news.

"He is risen. I have seen him. I have touched him. He is alive."

And so, too, is her hope.

In his triumph, Jesus could have paraded through the streets of Jerusalem. He could have knocked on Pilate's door. He could have confronted the high priest. But the first person our resurrected Lord appears to is a woman without hope. And the first words he speaks are, "Why are you crying?"

What a Savior we serve, or rather, who serves us. For in his hour of greatest triumph, he doesn't shout his victory from the rooftops. He comes quietly to a woman who grieves . . . who desperately needs to hear his voice . . . see his face . . . and feel his embrace.

PRAYER

 ear Risen Lord,

How hard it is to see clearly when devastating circumstances fill my eyes with tears. How blurry everything gets. Even you get blurry, and the sound of your voice becomes strangely unfamiliar.

Help me to blink away those tears to see that you are standing beside me, wanting to know why I am crying . . . wanting to know where it hurts . . . wanting to wipe away every tear from my eyes.

Thank you, Jesus, for being there, for never leaving me or forsaking me, even in the darkest and chilliest hours of my life.

From those circumstances that have shrouded my heart and entombed me, I pray that you would roll away the stone. It is too heavy and I am too weak to roll it away myself.

> Where there is doubt, roll away the stone and
> resurrect my faith.
> Where there is depression, cast aside the
> grave clothes and release my joy.
> Where there is despair, chase away the night
> and bring a sunrise to my hope.

Yet in my doubt, in my depression, in my despair, help me to continue to love you. Even if I don't understand how you are working in my life.

And I rejoice that no matter how dark the Friday or how cold the tomb, that with you as my risen Savior, there is always the warm hope of an Easter morning. . . .

A FINAL
INTIMATE MOMENT
WITH
PETER

SCRIPTURE

Afterward Jesus appeared again to his disciples, by the Sea of Tiberias. It happened this way: Simon Peter, Thomas (called Didymus), Nathanael from Cana in Galilee, the sons of Zebedee, and two other disciples were together. "I'm going out to fish," Simon Peter told them, and they said, "We'll go with you." So they went out and got into the boat, but that night they caught nothing.

Early in the morning, Jesus stood on the shore, but the disciples did not realize that it was Jesus.

He called out to them, "Friends, haven't you any fish?"

"No," they answered. He said, "Throw your net on the right side of the boat and you will find some." When they did, they were unable to haul the net in because of the large number of fish.

Then the disciple whom Jesus loved said to Peter, "It is the Lord!" As soon as Simon Peter heard him say, "It is the Lord," he wrapped his outer garment around him (for he had taken it off) and jumped into the water. The other disciples followed in the boat, towing the net full of fish, for they were not far from shore, about a hundred yards. When they landed, they saw a fire of burning coals there with fish on it, and some bread.

Jesus said to them, "Bring some of the fish you have just caught."

Simon Peter climbed aboard and dragged the net ashore. It was full of large fish, 153, but even with so many the net was not torn. Jesus said to them, "Come and have breakfast." None of the disciples dared ask him, "Who are you?" They knew it was the Lord. Jesus came, took the bread and gave it to them, and did the same with the fish. This was now the third time Jesus appeared to his disciples after he was raised from the dead.

When they had finished eating, Jesus said to Simon Peter, "Simon son of John, do you truly love me more than these?"

"Yes, Lord," he said, "you know that I love you."

Jesus said, "Feed my lambs."

Again Jesus said, "Simon son of John, do you truly love me?"

He answered, "Yes, Lord, you know that I love you."

Jesus said, "Take care of my sheep."

The third time he said to him, "Simon son of John, do you love me?"

Peter was hurt because Jesus asked him the third time, "Do you love me?" He said, "Lord, you know all things; you know that I love you."

Jesus said, "Feed my sheep. I tell you the truth, when you were younger you dressed yourself and went where you wanted; but when you are old you will stretch out your hands, and someone else will dress you and lead you where you do not want to go." Jesus said this to indicate the kind of death by which Peter would glorify God. Then he said to him, "Follow me!"

John 21:1–19

MEDITATION

What do you do when you've failed a friend? After you've cried till you're numb. After you've replayed the failure over and over in your mind. After you've run yourself down and can't think of any more names to call yourself. What do you do then?

You find some way to hold back the pain.

"I'm going fishing."

Peter is tired of thinking. He's tired of the incriminating conversations he's had with himself. He wants a mindless diversion, an escape.

But the sea is unsympathetic. And the night refuses him a reprieve.

In the melancholy darkness Peter is lulled by the rhythmic slapping of waves against the boat. His mind ebbs nostalgically back . . . back . . . back to when Jesus was in the boat with them and calmed the storm . . . back to when he walked on the water . . . back to when . . . .

Thus he passes the night away, throwing out his net and catching only slippery moments from the past.

Memories. That's all he's got now. But one of those memories he wishes he could throw back: how he stood there when Jesus needed him the most . . . stood there and denied even knowing him . . . cursed and swore and, and . . .

And then he hears a voice like a smooth stone skipping out to him from the shore. A faintly familiar voice.

"Throw your net on the right side of the boat and you

will find some fish."

The words jostle a sleeping memory. As soon as Peter throws out his net, the water churns with fish. And as the net fills up, his memory wakes to a strikingly similar morning three and a half years ago.

It was the morning Jesus first called him to be a disciple. He and his partners were cleaning their nets after they had fished all night and caught nothing. As they did, they listened to Jesus preaching on the seashore. He remembers when Jesus finished how he told him to row out to the deep water and let down the nets. The catch was so incredible the nets began to break and the boat started sinking. He remembers how he realized then that Jesus was Lord. And he remembers how unworthy he felt to be in his presence. He remembers pleading with Jesus to leave him. But Jesus didn't leave. Instead, he said that from now on they would be catching men. And the next three and a half years made that catch of fish look like a handful of minnows.

It's a precious memory—the dearest one to Peter's heart. And the Lord, so sensitive, stages the entire scene just for him. From the empty-handed night to the net full of fish. It's all for an audience of one—Peter.

As Peter works the net, reliving the memory, it suddenly dawns on John.

"It is the Lord!"

What do you do when you've failed a friend? You go to him.

Peter can't constrain himself. He throws himself into the water, and for a hundred yards his tears mingle with the sea. The memory has done its work.

Wet and shivering, Peter reaches the shore. His eyes look down to the warm charcoal fire. A similar fire had warmed him the night of his denial. His approach is suddenly tentative and uncertain. He agonizes over that night as he presses his palms toward the heat. He yearns to talk, but the chatter of his teeth cuts his words short.

Smoke curls above the fire, entwining his thoughts into a tangle as the disciples land on the shore and join them for breakfast. They, too, are timid and quietly eat and listen. After the meal, Jesus takes Peter aside. What he says is remarkable. What he doesn't say is even more so.

He doesn't say: "Some friend you turned out to be. . . . I'm really disappointed in you. . . . You let me down. . . . You're all talk. . . . Coward. . . . Boy, was I ever wrong about you. . . .And you call yourself a disciple?"

Instead, he asks simply, "Do you love me?" He asks three times, once for each denial. Not to rub it in, but to give Peter an opportunity to openly confess his love. By the third time Jesus asks him, Peter gets the connection, and a flame leaps to burn him from that smoldering memory.

But Jesus is not there to inflict pain; he is there to relieve it. Jesus had seen his bitter tears when the rooster crowed. That was all he needed to see. That was repentance enough. Peter looks up, longing for the faintest glimmer of forgiveness. And in a language beyond words, in a language of love, it glows from the Savior's eyes.

"Feed my sheep, Peter." Jesus' way of saying, "I still believe in you . . . I still think you're the right man for the job."

And with the words "Follow me," the restoration is complete. The painful memory is healed. Three and a half years ago Jesus asked Peter to follow him. The offer still stands, despite Peter's failure.

Jesus had orchestrated everything to bring back two memories to Peter's mind—a precious memory and a painful one. The painful one he brought back not to rebuke Peter but to restore him. He didn't want to make him grovel in the dirt. He didn't want to show him how right he was and how wrong Peter was. He brought it to the surface for one purpose and one purpose only—to heal it. To heal it so Peter could go on loving him and serving him without that painful memory leaning over his shoulder the rest of his life, wagging an accusatory finger.

That intimate moment proved to be a turning point in Peter's life. Within seven weeks, he would preach the boldest sermon of his life. It would be in Jerusalem, the very bastion of hatred against Jesus. Three thousand would be saved. They would form the nucleus of the church he would establish there.

Later, he would stand before Caiaphas himself and the entire ruling council that had conspired against Christ. He would stand up to them in a bold confession for his Savior. And he would go on preaching about his crucified Lord, shaking the foundations of the temple and sending a tremor to rock even the mighty pillars of the Roman Empire.

Finally, as Jesus said, he would be crucified. Eusebius tells us that when they were putting Peter on the cross, he asked to be crucified upside down for he didn't feel worthy to die in the same manner his Lord had.

What kind of friend inspires devotion like that?

A friend who prayed for him when he was weak. A friend who forgave him when he failed. A friend who healed a painful memory. A friend who loved him. A friend who believed in him.

A friend like Jesus.

A friend who first laid down his life for him.

PRAYER

ear Lord Jesus,

Thank you that no matter how miserably I have let you down, you are always there to pick me up. No matter how many times I have failed you, you are always there to forgive me. No matter how far I have drifted, you are always there on the shore, waiting for me to return—waiting with a comforting fire, warm food, and an affirming arm to put around my shoulder.

I thank you, too, Lord, for how you arrange the circumstances in my life to restore me. How you bring back the precious memories of a time when my love for you was so pure and intense. And how you gently recall to my mind the painful memories that need to be brought to the surface and healed.

I love you for so many reasons, Jesus. I love you for calling me to follow you. I love you for the honor you have bestowed on me to labor with you in building your kingdom. I love you for teaching me so much. I love you for being so patient when I am so slow to learn. I love you for the great friend you are to me.

I love you for all that I am because of you. I love you because with your tender hands you lift the crushed pile Satan leaves behind when he winnows, and you blow away the chaff. I love you that you don't focus on those husked failures but rather on the kernel, however small, of genuine love left in your palm. And seeing it, you take great delight.

Thank you for all the intimate moments we spend together. I know they mean as much to you as they do to me, and if the whole truth were known, probably more. It thrills me to know that I have contributed, even in a small way, to your divine pleasure. And that I can bring a smile to the face of God.

Help me to understand that only a few things really *are* necessary in life. And when you get right down to it, only one: to sit at your feet . . . listening . . . looking into your eyes . . . and loving you.

Thank you for the privilege of sitting at those nail-scarred feet. Grant me the grace never to regard that privilege casually, nor to neglect it, but to come there humbly, and to come there often. . . . because you are worthy to be adored, O beautiful Savior . . . because you are worthy to be adored. . . .

"Mary has chosen
what is better,
and it will not be
taken away from her."